Hans Byström

Finance
Markets, Instruments & Investments

Published by
Studentlitteratur AB
Lund, Sweden
www.studentlitteratur.se

 Copying prohibited

All rights reserved. No part of this publication may be reproduced or transmitted in any form or by any means, electronic or mechanical, including photocopying, recording, or any information storage and retrieval system, without permission in writing from the publisher.

Art. No 33042
ISBN 978-91-44-04891-8

© Hans Byström and Studentlitteratur 2007
www.studentlitteratur.se

Cover design by: Francisco Ortega
Cover illustration: Shutterstock

Printed in United States of America 2008
Lightning Source

To Camilla

Contents

Preface		**9**
1	**Introduction**	**11**
2	**Financial Institutions and Markets**	**17**
	2.1 Financial Institutions	18
	2.2 Financial Markets	21
	2.3 Summary	25
3	**Financial Arithmetic**	**27**
	3.1 Asset Returns	27
	3.2 Future Value Calculation – Compounding	29
	3.3 Present Value Calculation – Discounting	31
	3.4 Effective Annual Interest Rates	33
	3.5 Risky and Non-Risky Future Cash flows	36
	3.6 Summary	36
4	**Financial Instruments: Prices and Risks**	**39**
	4.1 The Law of One Price – Arbitrage	40
	4.2 Financial Risk – Important Concepts	44
	4.3 Financial Risk Measurement	47
	4.4 Financial Risk Management	52
	4.5 Summary	54
5	**Bonds (Debt)**	**57**
	5.1 Annuities	57
	5.2 Zero-Coupon Bonds	61
	5.3 Coupon Bonds	63
	5.4 Bond Prices, Time and Interest Rates	66
	5.5 Government Bonds versus Corporate Bonds	70
	5.6 Summary	72

6	**Stocks (Equity)**	**73**
	6.1 Dividends	73
	6.2 Pricing Stocks	75
	6.3 Stock Prices and Psychology – The Beauty Contest	80
	6.4 Fundamental Analysis versus Technical Analysis	81
	6.5 Summary	83
7	**Forwards and Futures**	**85**
	7.1 Forwards and Futures – The Basics	85
	7.2 Forwards and Futures – Risk Management Tools	89
	7.3 Forwards (Futures) Pricing	91
	7.4 Forwards and Futures – Predictors of Spot Prices?	94
	7.5 Summary	96
8	**Options**	**97**
	8.1 Some Background	98
	8.2 Options and Forwards – Similar but Different	100
	8.3 Basic Option Terminology	101
	8.4 Payoff Diagrams	107
	8.5 Put-Call Parity	114
	8.6 What Determines the Option Price?	118
	8.7 Option Pricing – The Black-Scholes Formula	122
	8.8 Summary	124
9	**Investment Portfolio Choice I:**	
	The Mean-Variance Framework	**125**
	9.1 Investment Portfolio Choice – The Basics	125
	9.2 Portfolio Returns, Risks and Correlations	127
	9.3 The Mean-Variance Framework	131
	9.4 Two-Fund Separation	142
	9.5 Summary	144
10	**Investment Portfolio Choice II:**	
	The Capital Asset Pricing Model (CAPM)	**145**
	10.1 CAPM – The Basics	145
	10.2 General Implications	148
	10.3 Risk Premiums on Risky Assets	152
	10.4 Portfolio Choice	154

	10.5 Stock Pricing	155
	10.6 Summary	157
11	**Market Efficiency**	**159**
	11.1 Are Markets Efficient?	159
	11.2 Weak Market Efficiency	162
	11.3 Semi-Strong Market Efficiency	166
	11.4 Strong Market Efficiency	167
	11.5 Stock Market Anomalies	167
	11.6 Summary	170
12	**Credit**	**171**
	12.1 Corporate Bonds	172
	12.2 Credit Rating Agencies	177
	12.3 The Basel II Regulatory Framework	180
	12.4 Credit Risk Models	182
	12.5 Credit Derivatives	185
	12.6 Summary	188
Appendix: Basic Mathematical Statistics		**191**
References		**201**
Subject Index		**203**

Preface

This introductory textbook in Finance is meant for courses in Finance, Economics or Business Administration. As such, it is also suitable for shorter Finance courses in Master's of Finance or MBA programs. Since it is written with a wide readership in mind, practitioners who need a basic understanding, or refreshment, of the core principles of Finance will also find it helpful.

To achieve the goal of writing a short and concise Finance textbook I have made an effort to minimize what (based on my teaching experience) students might perceive as excessive or repetitive. Since the level of mathematical analysis has been consciously kept to a minimum, readers will find that the book requires only the most elementary (high-school) mathematical and statistical concepts. The appendix at the end of the book contains the most important statistical concepts. It may well serve as a refresher for the more advanced readers at the same time as being a pointer for further studies, especially for readers with a weaker statistical background.

Finance, as an academic discipline, is often divided into Corporate Finance and Financial Markets (or Investments). This book focuses on the latter and the principal instruments traded there. Of course, the basic concepts behind rational investment strategies in these markets are also included. The material is up-to-date and, unlike typical introductory Finance textbooks, a chapter on Credit is included. Credit is a quickly growing segment (or asset class) of the financial world, meriting a place in any modern Finance textbook. It is quite likely that most introductory Finance textbooks will include such a chapter in the future.

I have taught introductory Finance to an array of Business, Economics, Government and Engineering students for many years at Lund University.

© The Author and Studentlitteratur

Finance – Markets, Instruments & Investments

This book is loosely based on notes prepared for these lectures, which hopefully means that answers to the most common student questions are given in the text. Furthermore, I have written many scientific articles on the very areas covered in this book, such as financial markets, bond prices, stock price predictions, asset price correlations, futures hedging, options pricing, credit risk modeling, credit derivatives, efficient markets, risk management and trading strategies. This will hopefully guarantee a presentation that is modern and in line with recent research findings.

I would like to thank Ola Jönsson and Hossein Asgharian for reading early versions of the book and Jaya Reddy for polishing my English. I would also like to thank the multitude of fellow lecturers and teaching assistants (Sonnie Carlsson, Rikard Green, Åsa Hansson, Per Hjertstrand, Mia Holmfeldt, Karl Larsson, Marcus Larson, Ola Larsson and Sirly Palenmark) at the Department of Economics at Lund University who have helped me teach this course through the years. Thanks for fruitful discussions on how to interpret and understand basic Finance!

Lund, August 2007
Hans Byström

1. Introduction

The point is, ladies and gentlemen, that: greed, for lack of a better word, is good. Greed is right; greed works. Greed clarifies, cuts through, and captures the essence of the evolutionary spirit. Greed, in all of its forms, greed for life, for money, for love, knowledge — has marked the upward surge of mankind and greed, you mark my words — will save not only Teldar Paper but that other malfunctioning corporation called the USA.

– Gordon Gekko ("Wall Street", the film)

Those working in *finance* are often portrayed as greedy, like the larger-than-life investment banker *Gordon Gekko* in the 1987 *Oliver Stone* movie *Wall Street*. In reality, however, regardless of any possible truth in the quote above, finance as a career choice or academic subject is far from just an arena for the pursuit of greed. In fact, it is one of the most important and productive areas of any market economy. For instance, without cheap and efficient recourse to finance, there would be little or no investments. And without investments, there would be no technological development. And without technological development, we would probably lead much shorter, duller and less fulfilled lives.

What is finance? Is there a clear and unambiguous definition of this very commonly-heard term? And is there a short and concise definition of the academic subject called finance (or financial economics)? Similarly, we often hear about financial markets, financial securities, financial invest-

© *The Author and Studentlitteratur*

Finance – Markets, Instruments & Investments

ments, financial plans, etc., but what is the actual meaning of the word *financial* in these expressions? Basically, what do the real-life versions of Gordon Gekko actually do in their corner offices on lower Manhattan or in the City of London? And what are all those professors at the finance department of your business school actually doing?

Unfortunately, it is not that easy to give a short and easily understandable definition that you can use when telling friends or family what you are currently studying at university. Or at least I have not found any definition that I am happy with. Somewhat depressingly, after more than ten years of studying, teaching, researching and writing about finance, and after more than fifteen years of investing in the financial markets, I still cannot explain to my friends what I am actually doing at work!

One, admittedly very general, definition describes finance as the subject that studies how individuals, companies and other organizations raise, allocate and use money and other assets over time for risky or non-risky ventures. According to another, more pragmatic, definition finance can simply be thought of as the subject that deals with all the institutions and markets that make up the *financial sector*. The financial sector, in turn, is one of the many (industrial) sectors that define a modern market economy. Examples of other sectors, besides the financial sector, are the health sector, that deals with prolonging or improving the life of people, the industry sector, that deals with producing products that we use to make our life comfortable, and the energy sector, that deals with producing the energy used in the other sectors. While most people know the roles played by the health sector or the energy sector in a market economy, far fewer know exactly what the financial sector does. Obviously, most people associate banks and insurance companies with the financial sector of the economy. At the same time, however, most people probably cannot explain what a modern bank or insurance company actually does. And even fewer can explain why we have a financial sector in the first place. For people with a basic financial education, however, the roles of banks and other players in the financial sector are quite clear. For them, in fact, it is obvious that the financial

12 © *The Author and Studentlitteratur*

Finance – Markets, Instruments & Investments

sector, in a way, is even more important than the other sectors. Simply put, without a properly working financial sector the other segments of the (market) economy would just not work very well.

More specifically, one of the most important roles of the financial sector is to channel funds in an efficient way from cash-rich individuals or organizations to cash-strapped ones. This is done either with the help of banks or through international debt and equity markets. In addition to the transfer of funds across time and regions, the financial sector also simplifies the transfer of risk from those who want to shed risk to those who want to expose themselves to risk. An insurance company is the epitome of such risk transferring, where it takes on risk from the insurance buyer in return for a fee. While these two roles of the financial sector are the more visual ones, the settling of payments between economical agents, the pooling of resources and the separation of ownership are examples of other important roles performed by financial markets and institutions. In essence, the financial sector of the economy (the financial system) is something of the grease that helps the wheels of the market economy turn with a minimum of friction.

> *Regardless of the exact definition of finance as a discipline, however, the purpose of this book is to give a short, but still complete, overview of the extremely important financial segment of the modern market economy. Particular emphasis will be put on the markets and instruments that can be found in the financial sector. In a way, the book will be my definition of finance.*

We conclude this introductory chapter with an example that raises many of the issues discussed throughout the book. A first look at the example might leave you slightly confused by all the unfamiliar terms.[1] My hope, nonetheless, is that you will fully understand the example after having read this book. If not, the fault is either yours or mine!

---

[1] The most important terms are marked in bold. The chapter where the term is discussed is also indicated.

© The Author and Studentlitteratur

Finance – Markets, Instruments & Investments

The Mother of all Examples:

Imagine that you are the Chief Investment Officer (CIO) of a **hedge fund** (chapter 2) called *Blue Mint,*[2] which means that you are responsible for the hedge fund's overall **investment portfolio choice** (chapter 9-10). Like all hedge funds, your fund has collected funds from investors who believe that you can manage their money better than anyone else. In total, you have collected $1 billion which makes your fund quite average in size. You, as the CIO of the fund, are charged with the responsibility of finding good investments. You are a skilled portfolio manager and you are therefore expecting to be handsomely compensated. You have a difficult job, though, and the investors behind your fund expect you to deliver **returns** (chapter 3) that beat the **market return** (chapter 10) without taking on too much **risk** (chapter 4). Your compensation is performance-based and like the typical hedge fund of today you charge a 20% performance fee on top of a 2% management fee, which means that your fund makes an annual $20 million plus 20% of any return above the **risk-free interest rate** (chapter 3). Historically[3], hedge funds have rewarded their managers handsomely and you expect to be no exception.[4]

A hedge fund gives you a very broad investment mandate and you as the investment manager can choose from a range of different investments, domestically as well as internationally. This is good for **diversification** (chapter 9) purposes but it also makes your life more complicated. In addition, you can **go long as well as short** (chapter 7) and you can take positions both in the **spot** market and in the **forward** (chapter 7) market.

---

[2] There are thousands of hedge funds and they bear any number of names. I have noticed, however, that several of them use the word "blue" in their name. I have no idea why that is and I have no idea if blue is actually a more common color to use in a hedge fund name than any other color.

[3] The concept of hedge funds is a fairly new one and their number has grown exponentially over the last decade. At the same time, however, one should remember that John Maynard Keynes (one of the greatest economists and thinkers of our times) ran something that was similar to a hedge fund (The Chest Fund) as early as the 1920s.

[4] In the City of London, there were allegedly more than 2500 employees in the

salary) in 2006. There is no reason to believe that the typical hedge fund manager made less than that. Rather the opposite.

Finance – Markets, Instruments & Investments

Fixed-income securities (chapter 5) can be mixed with **credit-risky instruments** (chapter 12), **stocks** (chapter 6), currencies and commodities. **Options contracts** (chapter 8) may be used for **speculation** (chapter 8) as well as for **hedging** (chapter 4) your other positions. Furthermore, if you believe that you have spotted a free lunch you are allowed to use all the different **derivatives contracts** (chapter 7) to profit from these **arbitrage** (chapter 4) opportunities.

For obvious reasons it is important that you manage your risk appropriately. If not, the fund might collapse and you might not be able to get a new job in the investment community. While this is the first and foremost reason for you to spend many good hours managing the risks of your investment portfolio, the rest of society has another reason for being wary of your risk management qualities. Since most hedge funds have a lot of business with the large international **investment banks** (chapter 2), your collapse could trigger **bankruptcies** (chapter 12) in these banks as well. In very unfortunate circumstances that could lead to a domino-like crisis where the collapsing bank(s) causes several other banks to fail as well. Such a **systemic crisis** (chapter 12) is not very likely but if we were to face one, we would not forget it in a hurry![5] The possibility of such a full-blown financial crisis being triggered by a major hedge fund collapse is one reason why some cry out for regulation of the hedge fund industry. Currently, hedge funds are much less **regulated** (chapter 12) by the **regulatory and supervisory agencies** (chapter 12) than ordinary banks and **mutual funds** (chapter 2). It should be added, though, that you as a hedge fund investor typically, but not necessarily, belong to the category of optimists. You do not expect a crisis such as the one pictured above to unfold.

Finally, one of the major arguments for your choice of starting the hedge fund is that you do not believe in the **efficient market hypothesis** (chapter 11). In other words, you expect to beat the performance of so-called **passive** (chapter 10) investors, even after the risk has been considered. You do not dismiss the **capital asset pricing model (CAPM)** (chapter 10) as nonsense, but you do not directly embrace the model either. By actively

---

[5] As recently as in the early 1990s, there were serious troubles in many European banking systems. There were even some examples of banks that collapsed (went bankrupt).

© *The Author and Studentlitteratur*

15

Finance – Markets, Instruments & Investments

managing your portfolio, you are convinced that you are one of the new masters of the universe, and that you will possibly be the Warren Buffett of the new millenium.[6]

---

[6] Warren Buffett, also known as the "Sage of Omaha", will not be the second richest man on the planet for much longer. The reason is not that the famous "old-economy" investor has lost his Midas touch. Instead, the reason is one of the noblest you can think of. The year 2006 was an important year for charity, since the 76-year-old Mr. Buffett decided to donate 83% of his fortune to a fund that tries to enhance healthcare in developing countries and reduce extreme poverty. And the best thing is yet to come: the fund he decided to donate his money to is the Bill and Melinda Gates Foundation. Mr. Buffett ignored any ego he might posses and simply put his money where he thought it could do most

Buffett ....

2. Financial Institutions and Markets

As mentioned in the previous chapter, the financial sector is a critical part of any modern market economy. The financial sector is made up of banks, insurance companies and other financial institutions in addition to the various financial markets found around the world. Financial institutions include small financial consultancy firms and stock broking firms as well as large multinational banks and asset management firms. The financial markets, in turn, include rather local markets such as the Icelandic real estate market or the Bolivian stock market as well as truly global markets such as the currency market or the crude oil market.

The reason for economical agents to turn to financial institutions or markets with their financial needs, instead of dealing directly with one another, is that it is less risky, less costly and more efficient. Whether the economical actors ultimately choose banks or markets to solve their problems, however, depends not only on the actors themselves but also on the economical environment where they are active. In this context one often hears that a certain country or economy is bank-based or market-based. Indeed, all countries have both banks as well as financial markets, but just how important are these segments of the financial system? In countries such as the US, UK or Sweden the financial markets are very well developed and these countries are labeled market-based economies (despite having some of the world's most developed banks). Other countries such as Japan and Germany also have highly developed financial markets. Notwithstanding, they are often named bank-based societies. What it all boils down to is how financial transactions,

© The Author and Studentlitteratur   17

Finance – Markets, Instruments & Investments

payments, and other financial decisions in the country are *mainly* done; through the banks or in the markets.

Countries such as Germany and the UK are very similar, in so far as their economies are concerned. Both economies are large, global and competitive and among the most advanced in the world. As a consumer, you can buy and sell pretty much the same things at the same time for pretty much the same price in the two countries. But for an investor, such as the hedge fund Blue Mint in chapter 1, the question of whether the economy is market-based or bank-based can be a very important one. We cannot go into detail here about the major implications of this divide, but we will at least try to explain the role and functioning of various financial institutions and markets. When you understand more about these concepts, you yourself can investigate whether your country is more or less bank-based than, say, the UK. And more importantly, you will understand a little bit more about this hard-to-define concept that we call finance.

2.1 Financial Institutions

This section introduces some of the more important financial institutions. The descriptions are deliberately short and their purpose is merely to simplify the reading of the rest of the book. The list is in no way complete and the exact definitions of the various institutions are under constant change.

– Banks

This is the prime example of a financial institution. Banks have "always" existed but their role has shifted somewhat over the centuries. While the traditional banking activity once might have been channeling funds from entities with surplus funds to those lacking funds, today's banks are involved in everything from this transfer of funds to stock broking and currency trading. Today, there are also many different kinds of banks, such as commercial banks, merchant

18   *© The Author and Studentlitteratur*

Finance – Markets, Instruments & Investments

what constitutes one type of bank or another differs from country to country. Furthermore, in many countries, the major banks are a combination of commercial, merchant and investment banks. For us, it suffices to think of a bank as a financial intermediary involved in all kinds of financial transactions. When a company wants to borrow money it can turn to a bank. When an individual wants to postpone consumption he or she can choose to deposit money with one or more banks. When investors want to buy or sell stocks they can do that through banks. Importantly, however, more and more of these tasks can also be performed by other institutions or perhaps even by markets. We will discuss this development in more detail below.

– Insurance Companies

When it comes to financial actors' desire to reduce risk, the insurance company is the obvious example of a financial institution enabling this. Insurance companies accept risk that other financial actors decide to shed. In doing so, they charge a fee, the insurance premium. There are insurance companies insuring property, cars and other physical objects and there are insurance companies insuring individuals against illness, injuries or death. Sometimes, all these insurance contracts are provided by the same company, and sometimes the insurance company is specialized in one or more lines of insurance. A common trait of most insurance companies, however, is that they are good at dealing with extreme but unlikely events. It should also be mentioned that banks and insurance companies sometimes exist under the same roof. These firms are called bancassurance firms. Finally, the insurance companies themselves occasionally buy insurance from other specialized, so-called, reinsurance firms.

– Investment Management Firms

This is a large and disparate group of firms involved in different stages of the investment process. Some firms (such as those that manage and administer *pension funds* and *mutual funds*) invest in widely traded assets, such as stocks, bonds and commodities, while other firms (such as *private equity firms* and *hedge funds*) invest in non-standard assets

© The Author and Studentlitteratur

19

Finance – Markets, Instruments & Investments

such as privately-held companies or more or less complicated derivatives securities. While the boundaries of the various investment firms are fairly blurry, what is common to all of them is that they buy assets they find undervalued and sell those that they find overvalued. In the process, they hope to make a profit. Most of these firms invest on behalf of someone else (the actual investor), and sometimes they use borrowed money to spice up the return (leverage). One of the most widely spread investment management firms is the *fund management firm*. These firms collect funds from the public (the investors are often private individuals such as you and me) and invest them in assets within a certain category or region such as bio-technology stocks or European government bonds. Typically, fund management firms spread their investments within one or more asset classes in order to reduce the risk and maximize the profit for the investor.

– Exchanges
The last financial institution to be treated here is the exchange (securities exchange). The reason why it is saved for last is its close link to the markets described in the next section. The reader is probably familiar with the concept of a stock exchange; the market-place where stocks are publicly traded. However, there is a long list of other exchanges such as commodity exchanges, futures exchanges or electricity exchanges, where all kinds of financial contracts (assets) are traded. The common theme, however, is that the exchange provides an organized marketplace for any good or service that is bought or sold in large enough quantities. Furthermore, to be traded on an exchange, the product has to be reasonably standardized. Otherwise, it is difficult to reach the volume needed to motivate exchange trading, and the trading is better done directly between the buyer and the seller without involving a third party. Off-exchange buying or selling of financial securities is called *over-the-counter* (OTC) trading.

There are of course numerous other financial institutions performing important tasks in the financial system. Some of the more important ones

20   © *The Author and Studentlitteratur*

Finance – Markets, Instruments & Investments

financial supervisory agencies (such as the Security and Exchange Commission (SEC) in the US), the credit rating agencies (such as Standard & Poor's or Moody's), the International Monetary Fund (IMF), the World Bank, the Bank for International Settlements (BIS), and the Development Banks (such as the Asian Development Bank (ADB)).

2.2 Financial Markets

In a way, a financial market is also an institution. Here, however, we treat a financial market as something substantially different from a financial institution. In fact, we treat the market as the opposite; a non-institutional means of servicing the financial community. The descriptions below are somewhat sketchy and we will come back to more rigorous discussions of the most important financial markets in later chapters.

– Debt Markets (Fixed Income)

When a government needs to borrow money it can turn to the debt market, which is the market for loans and where the main instrument traded is the government bond. When an investor buys a government bond he or she lends money to the government for a fixed period of time. In return, the investor gets a fixed, in advance known, interest rate (thereby the name fixed income). The investment is more or less risk-free since the government is not a credit risk, i.e. the investor knows with certainty that he/she will get the money back. There are bonds with a range of different lifetimes (maturities) that vary from as short as one month to as long as thirty years.

– Debt Markets (Credit)

Unlike the government, a bank or ordinary non-financial company that wants to borrow money in the capital market will have to convince the lender that it will be able to pay back the loan plus any interest rate payments. Due to the risk of non-payment (called credit risk), the borrower has to pay a higher interest rate than the government (the

© *The Author and Studentlitteratur*

sovereign). The difference is called the credit spread. The credit spread is what makes bonds issued by companies (corporate bonds) different to those issued by governments. Otherwise, corporate bonds are similar to bonds issued by governments. Over the last five to ten years the market for credit-risky instruments has grown tremendously, particularly the segment of the credit market that is called the credit derivatives market. The markets for credit default swaps (CDSs) and collateralized debt obligations (CDOs) are some of the fastest growing financial markets, and not only in the credit world.

– Equity Markets

The equity market is probably familiar to most readers. It is more widely known as the stock market and, basically, it is the market for company ownership. If you own a stock in a company, it simply means that you own a certain share of that company. If you own all the stocks issued by the company, then the company is all yours (after its debt, if any, has been repaid). As opposed to the fixed income market, the equity market is a very risky one; there is a non-insignificant probability of losing the entire investment, but as compensation you are likely to get a higher return on your investment than you would if you invested in the debt market. As a stockholder you are entitled to a yearly dividend, i.e. some of the profit is distributed among the stockholders. If the company is making a loss, it does not usually pay a dividend for that year. Just like the bond investor, the stockholder can never lose more than the invested amount.

– Foreign Exchange Markets

Except for a small group of academic economists (who promote a single global currency), most people find it natural for different countries to have different currencies. Although some countries share a currency, such as the Euro countries and the Euro, most countries have their own currency. Thus, each time a company buys something from a company in another country it has to pay in a foreign currency. Essentially, it has to buy the foreign currency and then make the purchase. Traditionally, these currency transactions were limited to

Finance – Markets, Instruments & Investments

international trade situations. With increasing capital market volumes, however, each purchase or sale of a foreign asset involves a currency transaction. Needless to say, the currency market is therefore an extremely important financial market. In fact, it is probably the largest market there is. Despite that, or perhaps because of that, we will not treat that market in this book. Currency markets are often treated in more macro-economically oriented finance textbooks. All we have to remember here is that each time we buy assets in foreign countries (for diversification purposes perhaps), we have to take currency fluctuations into consideration.

– Commodity Markets

If you think that assets such as stocks and bonds are concepts that are too abstract to attract your interest, perhaps commodities may cheer you up. Commodities are all real assets that you use for productive purposes or for consumption. Some of the most important ones are fossil fuels such as crude oil and natural gas, precious metals such as gold and silver, industrial metals such as nickel or copper and non-metals such as cotton and coffee. Just like stocks, these assets are often traded on exchanges, and many commodities are traded in huge volumes. Two of the most important commodities are oil and gold. As oil is used in many industrial processes and transportation, its price is an important determinant of the business cycle. Gold, in turn, is often considered a safe haven in times of crisis, due to its high intrinsic value; both as an input into important industrial processes and for its use in jewelry and other precious items.[7] As a result, the gold price often moves in the opposite direction to other financial assets, which may be good in crisis situations. There are tens of other types/families of commodities and each type has its own particularities. We therefore leave the discussion on commodities to more specific commodities books.

---

[7] Gold is clearly a scarce commodity. In fact, according to some estimates, if all the gold that has ever been refined (round) was collected and melted into a cube the side of the cube would be a mere 20m!

© *The Author and Studentlitteratur*

23

Finance – Markets, Instruments & Investments

– Forward and Futures Markets

When you buy foreign currency at the currency exchange desk of a bank or a stock on the stock exchange, you typically do that in the *spot market*, i.e., you pay now for immediate delivery. Sometimes, however, you want to know in advance what you have to pay for something in the future. For instance, airlines typically want to know in advance what they will have to pay for air fuel in the future. The way airlines, and other companies, solve this problem is by trading in the forward (or futures) market, where the buyer of the fuel decides on the terms of the purchase today but gets delivery at a certain, fixed, future point in time. Forward and futures contracts are available in most major asset classes, such as stocks, currencies and crude oil and natural gas. As is quite obvious, forward markets are perfect tools for risk reduction and evidence of their huge popularity is the fact that in some markets the forward market is actually larger than the underlying spot market. In addition to being used for risk management, forwards can also be used as an efficient tool to speculate on falling as well as rising market prices. Finally, forwards and futures are very similar and the exact differences between these two contract types will be treated in a later chapter.

– Options Markets

Just like forwards and futures, options were initially invented for risk management purposes. With time, however, they have also become popular for purely speculative purposes. The reason is that they give investors the opportunity to acquire huge amounts of *leverage* without the need to borrow funds. Obviously, nothing is free in the finance world and the increased leverage incurs an increased risk. Options have got their name from the option they give their owner. If you own a call option on a certain stock, it gives you the right to buy that stock at some time in the future at a pre-determined price. This option is clearly very useful for financial actors and options therefore have to be paid for. They are never given away for free. Finally, just like forwards, options are available in most major asset classes.

Finance – Markets, Instruments & Investments

– Real Estate Markets

Real estate, i.e. houses, apartments and other buildings, are becoming more and more commoditized. Even though houses are not traded on exchanges, the markets are large and sufficiently advanced to be considered an asset class on their own. Real estate, or property as it is sometimes called, can be divided into commercial and residential real estate. The former is made up of offices and factories and the latter of houses and apartments. Real estate markets are not as advanced as bond and stock markets, but many of the features of the more advanced markets are now being introduced in this market as well. Examples are futures contracts that enable investors to profit from falling as well as increasing house prices. Real estate is not typically treated in introductory finance books and we follow that tradition in this book.

2.3 Summary

This chapter has listed some of the more important financial *institutions* and *markets*. While this book mainly focuses on financial markets, it is nevertheless useful to be familiar with the most important financial institutions, such as banks and insurance companies. We have made a distinction between financial institutions and financial markets throughout the chapter. In a way, though, the market is an institution in its own right. Moreover, markets keep embracing, at a seemingly steadily increasing rate, areas of finance that were once taken care of by other institutions. Examples are credit risk management, corporate borrowing and electricity pricing.

© The Author and Studentlitteratur

3. Financial Arithmetic

It is often necessary to compare cash flows with each other, but the problem is that cash flows often come at different points in time. For instance, one might want to compare a future interest rate payment with a bank deposit today. If one wants to compare such cash flows, one first needs to transform them (in the time dimension) so that they are comparable. It is a bit like having to convert the US dollar price of an *iPod* into Japanese yen if you want to compare *iPod* prices in the US and in Japan. Or as the old saying goes, apples should be compared to apples, not to oranges.

In this chapter we will mainly discuss the *time value of money*; i.e. the well known fact that a dollar today is worth more than a dollar tomorrow. Only after having stated this observation in mathematical language can we start comparing cash flows at different points in time. First, though, we will define one of the most important concepts in finance; namely asset *returns*.

3.1 Asset Returns

Asset prices are central objects in the study of finance. If markets work satisfactorily, the market price of an asset (instrument, security) tells us the value of the asset, and this information is a key concept for any investor, whether he/she invests in oil, diamonds, biotech-stocks or government bonds. An equally important object, however, is the *percentage change* in the price of an asset from one point in time to another. This is called the *asset return* and is actually more often the object of study in financial models than prices.

© The Author and Studentlitteratur

Finance – Markets, Instruments & Investments

The return at time t, r_t, is defined as the percentage price change from time t to time $t+1$

$$r_t = \frac{P_{t+1} - P_t}{P_t} \qquad (3.1)$$

If t represents today and $t+1$ is next year, then r_t is simply the annual return effective from today. If the asset that we are studying is an ordinary stock, then we call the percentage change the stock return. Likewise, if the asset is the price of a ton of a certain quality of cacao, the percentage price change is simply called the cacao price return.

Assets such as stocks, cacao, oil, real estate, gold and vintage cars have one thing in common; they are so-called *risky assets*, which means that their future value is uncertain. Since we do not know for sure what our risky asset will be worth in, let's say, a year's time, the investment is of course a risky one and the return on the asset is risky (uncertain). If we take the purchase of a house, for instance, the owner does not know if the house will be worth more or less than his or her purchasing price when he or she is about to sell it. We will see in a later chapter that it is likely that the price of the house will go up over time (as compensation to the investor for taking on the risk), but the important point is that the investor can never be absolutely sure of it. He/she is exposed to financial (price) risk.

The other fundamental type of asset, besides the risky asset, is *the risk-free asset*. Contrary to the risky asset, the owner of a risk-free asset knows with 100% certainty what the value of the asset will be at any point in the future. The risk-free return is often called the *risk-free interest rate*. The holder of the risk-free asset is not exposed to price risk and he/she does not have to live with the uncertainty of, let's say, the real estate investor. Consequently, the risk-free interest rate will typically be lower than returns on houses or other risky assets. For the purposes of this book, the reader may think of the risk-free asset as

28   © *The Author and Studentlitteratur*

Finance – Markets, Instruments & Investments

savings in a bank account (at least as long as the bank is financially healthy and far from bankruptcy).

3.2 Future Value Calculation – Compounding

There are at least three reasons why one typically prefers receiving a dollar today to receiving a dollar tomorrow:

- you can earn interest on your dollar (due to the time value of money)
- you can probably buy less for one dollar tomorrow than today (due to inflation)
- you are typically happier with actually having the dollar in your pocket now than with a mere promise of having the dollar in your pocket tomorrow (due to uncertainty)

The role of uncertainty will be treated in later chapters and the role of inflation is beyond the scope of this book. Instead, in this section we focus solely on the *time value of money*. We will learn to calculate the future value of a cash flow today as well as the present value of a cash flow in the future.

The future value of a certain cash flow today is easily calculated using so-called *compounding*. If we assume that the annual interest rate is 5%, then an investment of $1 today grows to $1.05 in one year's time since

$$1 \cdot (1 + 0.05) = 1.05 \tag{3.2}$$

This way of compounding is called simple compounding. There are alternative ways of compounding (see below), but in this book we will solely use simple compounding.

We can now go on to calculate the future value of the initial $1 investment in two years' time. Since the value has grown to $1.05 after one year it is easy to accept that the value after two years is equal to $1.1025

© The Author and Studentlitteratur

29

$$1.05 \cdot (1 + 0.05) = 1.1025 \tag{3.3}$$

If we continue in the same fashion we end up with the following series of future values of $1 today

The future value in one year = $1.05
The future value in two years = $1.1025
The future value in three years $\approx$ $1.1576
The future value in four years $\approx$ $1.2155

.

.

We may of course generalize the method by applying this procedure over and over again as follows

$$FV = PV \cdot (1 + r)^n \tag{3.4}$$

where FV is the future value, PV is the present value, r is the rate of compounding (the interest rate) and n is the future date at which we want to calculate the future value of our initial cash flow.

We end this chapter on compounding with an example.

Example 3.1
Let us assume that you have managed to save $10000 and that you want to know how much this amount will have grown in four years' time when you graduate from university. If we assume that the (risk-free) interest rate that you earn on your savings account in your local bank is 2%, then the future value of your $10000 in four years' time will be

$$FV = PV \cdot (1 + r)^n = \$10000 \cdot (1 + 0.02)^4 \approx \$10824$$

since $r = 0.02$, $n = 4$ and $PV = \$10000$. In other words, your savings will have grown by $800 or so in those four years. Not a very significant wealth

Finance – Markets, Instruments & Investments

increase you might think. And then we have not even considered the fact that most prices will probably have gone up in those four years as well (due to inflation). Do not despair, for there is a way of boosting your return; invest at a higher interest rate! If the rate were 6% instead, the future value would be

$$FV = \$10000 \cdot (1 + 0.06)^4 \approx \$12625$$

In this case you would see your savings increase by more than 25%. This is clearly a healthy improvement over the earlier 8%. And if the interest rate was a whopping 18% the future value would be

$$FV = \$10000 \cdot (1 + 0.18)^4 \approx \$19388$$

That is, your savings would almost double in value. The lesson, as may be seen from this simple example, is that the rate of compounding has a significant effect on the end result. This is particularly true if you are saving for a long period of time. If you are 20 years old and if you (or perhaps your parents) had put $10000 in the high-interest rate banking account above when you were born, the value of the $10000 would have been an astonishing $274000 today (a sum that could buy a nice house in most countries). There is only one problem with this example; risk-free interest rates are rarely as high as 18%. Actually, to get an annual return as high as 18% you would most likely have to invest in something considerably riskier than a savings account. Not even an ordinary stock portfolio delivers that kind of annual return, consistently, over a time period as long as 20 years.

3.3 Present Value Calculation – Discounting

When pricing stocks, bonds and many other financial securities it is often necessary to calculate the present value of one or more future cash flows. This is the exact opposite of what we did in section 3.2 and is done by simply solving for *PV* in equation (3.4). A slight reorganization of equation (3.4) gives the present value formula

© *The Author and Studentlitteratur*

Finance – Markets, Instruments & Investments

$$PV = \frac{FV}{(1+r)^n} \tag{3.5}$$

where *PV* is the present value of the future cash flow *FV*. *r* is now called the rate of discounting (the interest rate) and *n* is the time to the future cash flow. This formula for present value calculation, or *discounting*, is used over and over again, both in this book and in finance in general.

An example shows how the formula is used.

Example 3.2

Let us pretend that it is 2007 and that you are the mayor of the city of Budapest. Furthermore, we assume that Budapest has been chosen to organize the 2016 Olympic Games. This means that any income generated by the Games will come in nine years' time. Clearly, the city of Budapest has had to make some huge immediate infrastructure investments and you have found out that these investments amount to around 1 billion Euro. In order to be able to compare these immediate outlays to the future income generated by ticket sales etc. you need to calculate the present value of this future income (remember the discussion about apples and oranges above). Let us for the sake of simplicity assume that you know for sure that this future income will be 1 billion Euro (perhaps some financial firm has guaranteed you this amount, no matter what the actual sales are). If we further assume that the risk-free annual interest rate in Hungary (where Budapest is the capital) is 4%, the present value of this sum is easily calculated using our present value formula

$$PV = \frac{FV}{(1+r)^n} = \frac{1000000000}{(1+0.04)^9} \approx 702587000 \, \text{Euro}$$

since *r = 0.04, n = 9* and *FV = 1000000000*. As the mayor of Budapest, you are a bit concerned, because you had thought of the income as 1 billion Euro and not 700 million Euro. Of course, in doing so you made a serious mistake. You cannot compare future incomes to present costs without first calculating the present value of the future cash flow. If you have total costs of more than 702587000 Euro this year (which you clearly have), these

Finance – Markets, Instruments & Investments

outlays are actually larger than the present value of the income. This is not good!

Why? Well, imagine that you had to borrow 1 billion Euro today for the initial outlays. This loan would then grow to a much higher amount than 1 billion Euro in nine years time (1423311812 Euro) and your future income of 1 billion Euro would not be enough to repay your loan. As an alternative way of convincing yourself that you have to calculate the present value before comparing a future cash flow to current cash flows, you can think about how much 1 billion Euro would grow in nine years if you could put it in a bank account (at 4% interest) instead of using it for infrastructure investments. Of course, in nine years this sum would have grown to 1423311812 Euro and you would have been substantially richer than today. This alternative use of the money should not be forgotten; it is why one Euro of income tomorrow is always worse than one Euro of income today. Finally, note that you would have an easier life as mayor of Tokyo. In Japan, the risk-free interest rate has been close to zero for the last couple of years and present values and future values are essentially the same.

3.4 Effective Annual Interest Rates

One interesting effect of compounding is that it makes investments, or loans for that matter, grow faster than you might expect from a first somewhat hasty observation. We saw the effect of this in section 3.2; a seemingly small change in interest rate had a significant effect on the future amount. The reason for this is that not only the initial deposit grows as a result of the positive interest rate; the interest rate payment from previous periods does so as well, i.e. you get *interest on interest*.

Pretend that you have borrowed $1000 to buy a flat-screen TV, using a loan from the consumer electronics shop itself. The shop charges an annual interest rate of 18% on a monthly basis. If the annual interest rate is 18%, then the monthly interest rate is of course 1.5% (18/12). Now, since the interest rate (1.5% of $1000) is added to your debt each month, your debt is actually growing faster than you might have thought at first. *How* fast is it growing on a yearly basis? Or stated differently, what is the actual, or *effective*, annual interest rate? To answer that question we

© The Author and Studentlitteratur

33

Finance – Markets, Instruments & Investments

turn to our future value formula above, which immediately gives us the size of the $1000 debt in one year's time as

$$FV = 1000 \cdot (1 + 0.015)^{12} = \$1195.6$$

Your debt has not grown at a yearly pace of 18% but rather at a pace of 19.56%! In other words, your effective annual interest rate is 19.56% as a result of the interest rate being added to your debt once a month instead of once a year. The frequent compounding obviously magnifies your debt. And if you were not trained in financial analysis you would think that you were being cheated by the consumer electronics shop. Now, however, you know better, and as long as the consumer electronics shop informed you that the interest rate was compounded monthly they did nothing wrong. They just made some money from your reluctance to wait with your consumption until you had the money in your pocket.

It is quite normal to face rates of compounding other than yearly, and a common example is a bank account where your interest rate is added to your account each week, month or quarter instead of on a yearly basis. Now that you are saving money you are happy about the effect of compounding since the magnification works in both directions; if two banks offered you a 3% interest rate but one of the banks, *alfa*, offered you monthly compounding and another, *beta*, offered you yearly compounding, then you would obviously choose the bank *alfa*.

The method can be formulized as follows

$$EFF = \left[1 + \frac{SIMP}{n}\right]^{n} - 1 \qquad (3.6)$$

where *EFF* is the effective annual interest rate, *SIMP* is the so-called simple interest rate (the one you find in the business section of news-papers and advertisements for consumer electronics shop), and n is the compounding frequency.

Finance – Markets, Instruments & Investments

An example shows how the formula is used.

Example 3.3
If we apply the formula for the effective annual interest rate to the example
with the TV we end up with

$$EFF = \left[1 + \frac{0.18}{12}\right]^{12} - 1 = 0.1956$$

Of course, we get the same result as when we used the less formalized
formula earlier. If we repeat the whole exercise with different compounding
frequencies we get the following table.[8]

SIMP %	n	EFF %
18	1	**18**
18	2	18.81
18	4	19.25
18	12	**19.56**
18	52	19.68
18	365	19.72
18	∞	$e^{0.18} - 1 = 19.72$

As seen in this example, ordinary simple interest rates do not give you
enough information. They need to be complemented with the compounding frequency to give you meaningful information about the pace
at which your loan or investment will grow. Effective returns, on the

---

[8] Even if the compounding frequency goes to infinity the effective annual
interest rate does not turn infinite. There is a limit to how high the value of the
effective interest rate can be at a certain level of simple interest rate. This limit
is called the continuously compounded interest rate. We will not use such a
frequent compounding in this book, but continuous compounding is quite often
used in financial modeling. For the interested reader it may be mentioned that
the expression $[1 + 0.18/n]^n$ is equal to the exponential function $e^{0.18}$ in the limit
as n goes to infinity. This makes continuous compounding mathematically very
attractive.

© The Author and Studentlitteratur

Finance – Markets, Instruments & Investments

other hand, contain all the information you need without any additional information on compounding frequency.

3.5 Risky and Non-Risky Future Cash Flows

The discussion above always assumed that the future cash flows were known in advance. That is, there was no uncertainty regarding the actual size of the future cash flow. In some situations, however, we do not know in advance how large the cash flow will be; i.e. we have to make an intelligent guess, or estimate, as we usually call it in finance. In such cases the present value calculation is not as straightforward as demonstrated above. While the risk-free interest rate may be used when the cash flows are known in advance, a risk-adjusted interest rate has to be used when the present value of a *risky* cash flow is calculated.

We will not go into detail here about how the risk-adjustment is done. One widely accepted method will be described in chapter 10, but here it is sufficient to state the basic rule:

The more uncertain (or risky) the future cash flow is, the higher the risk-adjusted discount rate should be when calculating the cash flow's present value.

3.6 Summary

A basic concept that is used in all areas of finance is *the time value of money*, i.e. the fact that a dollar today is worth more than a dollar tomorrow. In this chapter we have studied this concept in some detail and we have learnt to discount and compound cash flows. The effective annual interest rate is another basic, but very important, concept described in this chapter. The real-life importance of effective interest rates as a phenomenon is a consequence of the well known fact that *money makes money and the money that money makes makes more money*! Finally, we have defined another very important finance concept in this chapter; the asset *return*. The return of an asset is the same as the

Finance – Markets, Instruments & Investments

percentage price change of the asset, and asset returns are as common in financial models as asset prices.

4. Financial Instruments: Prices and Risks

A central theme in finance is the pricing of various financial assets.[9] Sometimes the pricing is easily done by ordinary mortals, and sometimes it requires tens of "rocket scientists" or other highly skilled professionals (typically, banks hire Ph.D.s in mathematics, physics or finance to solve the most difficult pricing problems). In this chapter we will discuss the most important principle to follow when pricing financial assets and instruments; the *law of one price*. We will use this principle over and over again throughout this book.

Another central concept in finance is that of (financial) risk. The risk of a financial instrument is closely related to its price and in this chapter we will describe the most common way of quantifying financial risk, i.e. the *volatility*.[10] We will also introduce the main techniques of managing financial risk, a topic which will be treated more extensively in chapters 7–10.

---

[9] Other names for financial assets are financial securities or financial instruments.

[10] In chapter 10 we will introduce an alternative, but almost as important, measure of risk called the β-value (*beta*).

© The Author and Studentlitteratur

4.1 The Law of One Price – Arbitrage

The law of one price states that identical assets should have identical prices. This "law" is not a law, as such, but rather a reasonably likely state of the world. The process that leads to this state, i.e. the state where identical assets have identical prices, is called *arbitrage*. The law of one price is therefore often called the *arbitrage principle*.

Obviously, the pricing of financial assets and instruments is central to finance. Whether you are about to buy a stock on the London Stock Exchange or sign a complex insurance contract with an insurance company, you need to decide on a reasonable price of the stock or insurance contract. Otherwise, it is likely that the counterparty of the agreement will take advantage of your lack of information/knowledge and charge you too high a price. The most natural way of finding the price of a particular asset is to go to the marketplace and see what the current market price is. Unfortunately, this is only possible for the more standardized financial assets, such as exchange traded stocks and currencies.[11] If there is no observable price on the particular asset that you want to buy or sell, you are often limited to comparing the asset to other *similar* assets in order to infer a reasonable price. Moreover, if you are lucky, there might be other, seemingly different, but actually *identical* assets available in the marketplace. The law of one price then states that your asset and the identical one should trade at the same price in the market. Thus, you may determine your asset's price by simple comparison.[12]

---

[11] And, even in this case, there is a possibility that the price does not correctly represent the true value of the asset. Even in large efficient markets the price of an asset is sometimes too high or too low compared to its fundamental value. In this case it is useful to have another way of determining the proper price.

[12] More advanced (exotic) products are also typically priced using the law of one price. Modern (structured) financial products are often combinations of two or more basic assets, such as a bond and a stock option, and the price of such structured products is then simply the sum of the components' prices; remember, the prices of identical assets should always be identical.

Finance – Markets, Instruments & Investments

The law of one price (the arbitrage principle) is one of the most important concepts of finance, useful not only when determining the prices of proper financial assets such as bonds, options or gold, but also when determining interest rates and exchange rates. A smart use of this principle is of significant importance, and in this book we will return to the arbitrage principle when pricing basic financial instruments such as bonds, forwards and options. When applying the arbitrage principle, one has to be very careful, though. It is of crucial importance that the assets that are compared to each other are truly 100% identical. As an example, for a visitor to the (hypothetical) Royal Museum of Liberal Ideas in Stockholm a 5 SEK coin (the Swedish currency is krona, SEK) is not worth the same as five 1 SEK coins! The reason is that in order to enter the museum you have to put your bags in a locker for which you need exactly one 5 SEK coin. In this case, whether you have five or five hundred 1 SEK coins does not matter. Without a 5 SEK coin there is no way that you can enter the museum (unless you leave your bags in an unlocked locker, that is). As you correctly imagine, the typical visitor is prepared to pay more than 5 SEK for the 5 SEK coin, so we are *not* dealing with identical assets in this example. That is why the 5 SEK coin is suddenly worth more than five 1 SEK coins to the museum visitor. In other words, this is *not* an example where the law of one price breaks down. It is just not applicable.

Assets that are truly identical (with identical cash flows) should also trade at the same price in a well functioning market. If not, investors whose main role is to discover mispricings in the market, so-called *arbitrageurs*, will exploit the anomaly. They will simply buy the cheaper asset and sell the expensive one, and since the two assets are in fact identical, this strategy is 100% risk-free. Despite this the arbitrageur will earn a return that is higher than the risk-free return. This activity is called *arbitrage*.

© *The Author and Studentlitteratur*

Example 4.1

Wholesale tobacco can be bought all over the world, but is it possible for the price of a certain quality of tobacco to be priced differently in different places? For instance, if one ton of high quality Haitian tobacco costs $1500 in Paris, is the situation where the same tobacco costs $1700 in San Francisco sustainable? The answer is that it depends! Clearly, if there were no transaction costs associated with transporting the tobacco from Paris to San Francisco, then the price would have to be the same at both destinations. Otherwise, arbitrageurs, or other well informed tobacco traders, would buy the tobacco in Paris, transport it and sell it in San Francisco *and make a healthy profit without taking a risk.* In reality transporting a ton of tobacco across the Atlantic is not without cost, and depending on the actual costs it is possible for the prices of the same tobacco to differ. For instance, if the costs (transport, insurance, taxes etc.) sum up to $200, it is perfectly possible for the prices to be $1500 in Paris and $1700 in San Francisco. The law of one price is *not* violated. If, however, the transaction costs are lower than $200, then it is possible for a trader to buy the tobacco in Paris, transport it to San Francisco and sell it at a profit. The trader will not be alone in realizing this opportunity and, when more and more arbitrageurs follow the same trading strategy, the price of tobacco will be pushed upwards in Paris (the demand goes up) and downwards in San Francisco (the supply goes up). In the end, the price differential will be exactly equal to the transaction costs.

In fact, the arbitrageurs and the other well-informed tobacco traders, in the example above, provide all of us with a service. By buying and selling tobacco according to the example (arbitrage trading), they make the global tobacco market more efficient by forcing mispricings to quickly disappear. Like oil in a piece of machinery, the arbitrageurs grease the tobacco market through their hunt for arbitrage possibilities. And when sufficiently many arbitrageurs are involved in the arbitrage activities (surprisingly few arbitrageurs are in fact needed to move prices), the arbitrage opportunities quickly disappear. The market is said to have become *efficient*, i.e. all *free lunches* have disappeared. Another way of expressing the same thing is through the famous analogy that there cannot possibly be any hundred dollar bills lying on the sidewalk. If there had been, they would already have been picked up! Throughout

Finance – Markets, Instruments & Investments

the major part of this book we will assume that there are no such free lunches.

The arbitrage principle is important enough to merit another example.

Example 4.2[13]

A farmer is waiting at a bus stop and asks an economics professor, who is waiting for the bus as well, if he wants to play a game in which the farmer asks the professor a question and if the professor is unable to answer the question he has to give the farmer a dollar. Then, the professor asks the farmer a question, and if the farmer is unable to answer that question, he has to give the professor a dollar.

"Ok", says the professor, "but I have to warn you that I am an economics professor". The farmer replies that in this case they have to change the rules; if the farmer answers his question he will still receive a dollar, but if the professor answers his question he will only receive fifty cents. The professor agrees to these terms; he is after all an educated man and better trained to answer tricky questions.

The farmer starts, and he asks the question "what goes up the hill on seven legs and comes down the hill on three legs?" After some thinking the economics professor replies "I have no idea......what does go up the hill on seven legs and down the hill on three legs?" "Well", the farmer replies, "I don't know either. But if you give me my dollar I will give you your fifty cents!"

This example is supposed to illustrate the principle of arbitrage. That is, the activity of arranging a transaction involving a zero cash outlay that still generates a risk-free positive profit. In this example, the farmer was the arbitrageur and the "free lunch" was the fifty cents he kept after paying the professor his share!

---

[13] The example is slightly modified compared to the original story by Hal R. Varian in *Economic Perspectives*, 1 (2), 1987, pp. 55-72.

© *The Author and Studentlitteratur*

Finance – Markets, Instruments & Investments

4.2 Financial Risk – Important Concepts

When deciding to buy a stock, you are (hopefully) aware of the financial risk you are taking, i.e. the *risk* that the stock price might fall in the future.[14] Moreover, you probably know that the risk is larger than depositing your money in a savings account in a major bank or buying a government bond. Government bonds and bank accounts are usually assumed to be risk-free. Bonds and stocks will be treated in later chapters but even at this point it might be useful to ponder upon the risks associated with owning financial securities. The rest of this chapter will therefore present a broad overview of financial risk measurement and risk management. In addition, the examples will typically assume that the investor is exposed to the risks associated with owning a simple financial security such as a stock issued by a stock company. However, the concept is the same, regardless of whether the investor has bought a stock, a bond, real estate, gold or something else with an uncertain future price.

Most of us prefer a life without risks, at least if we are not adequately compensated for bearing the risk. According to economists, we (Homo Economicus) are *risk-averse*. Studies of individuals making choices under uncertainty have repeatedly shown that most individuals are risk-averse, and most financial models are based on this widely accepted "truth". If you want to know whether you, yourself, are risk-averse or not, consider the following thought experiment. In an unusual (hypothetical) lottery called *phiffty-phiffty* there is a 50-50 chance of winning $25000 or $75000. Moreover, the lottery ticket is for free (do not ask me why)! Would you choose to take part in this lottery or be given a $50000 gift to put straight into your pocket? If you, like me, choose the latter alternative, you are a typical risk-averse individual. If, on the other hand, you are in doubt, consider the following small change to the experiment; instead of $25000 and $75000, the lottery prizes have been changed to $0 and $100000. Again, the average prize is the same,

---

[14] The possibility that the stock could rise in the future should not be categorized as *risk*. This is better described as *chance*.

44   *© The Author and Studentlitteratur*

Finance – Markets, Instruments & Investments

$50000, as the certain gift. Would you still choose to take part in the lottery? If the answer is yes, you are a true *risk-lover*. If, on the other hand, you consider the two alternatives as equally good, economists would call you *risk neutral*. Finally, if, like me and most other people, you prefer the certain gift, you are *risk-averse*.

Regardless of whether you are actually risk-averse or not, the rest of this book will assume that you are, and, as a consequence of your *risk aversion*, that you are prepared to pay to avoid risk. Or put differently, if you can choose between two alternatives with equal payoff, you choose the one with the lower risk, as shown in the lottery example above.[15] In any case, as a consequence of the general public's risk aversion, reducing one's risk exposure will always incur a cost, whether it is money, time, energy, peace of mind or something else. As an example, if you want to reduce the risk of not passing your introductory finance exam, you had better study more intensively and attend all the lectures. In any case, you realize that it brings a cost to you. It might not be one that can be measured in dollars (even though it could be, since each extra hour spent in the class room is one hour less to spend earning money somewhere else) but it could cost you your good mood if you do not like finance, or it could cost you a backache, if you have to sit too much. Another common situation where the reduction of risk bears a cost is when you choose between putting your money in the vault versus in (risky) stocks. Here, the cost is simply the return that you lose when putting your money in the (risk-free) vault. Simply put, risk reduction is costly![16]

Regardless of whether you are risk-averse or not, you are always exposed to various risks. The risks can be non-financial, such as the risk of dying of lung-cancer from too much smoking, or financial, such as

---

[15] In fact, the amount you are prepared to pay to avoid a certain risk can be used as a measure of your risk aversion.

[16] I can only come up with one strategy to reduce your risk at no cost; *diversification*. We will come back to this subject several times in this book. It is sometimes said that *diversification is the only free lunch* in the market.

© *The Author and Studentlitteratur*

Finance − Markets, Instruments & Investments

having to sell your house at a far lower price than you bought it for. Smoking can be avoided, but financial risks are typically harder to avoid. One nice feature of financial risks though, which some non-financial risks do not have, is that they can be transferred to someone else. The prime example is a typical insurance product where you transfer the risk to an insurance company for a fee. You have bought risk reduction! More generally, as we will see in section 4.4, there are three related but fundamentally different ways of reducing one's financial risk; *hedging*, *insurance* and *diversification*. We will talk extensively about each of these three approaches in later chapters.

Another interesting property of risk, non-financial as well as financial, is that a certain risky investment or activity may often be considered more risky by one individual than by another. Consider a wealthy Dutch dentist and an equally wealthy Dutch stockbroker who both consider investing a large share of their savings in a portfolio of Dutch stocks. Obviously, this particular investment is much more risky for the stock-broker. The reason is that if the stock market crashes, the stockbroker will lose both his/her job and his/her savings.[17] The dentist, on the other hand, will at least continue working as usual after the crash as if nothing had ever happened. The implication is that the risk of an investment cannot be evaluated in isolation. The rest of the investor's particular risk exposure has to be considered as well. This important observation has to be remembered in later chapters when we talk about investment strategies.

---

[17] Of course, if the stock market booms, instead, the stock broker will be richer both as a result of the increased value of his stock portfolio and from a (likely) higher stock broking salary and bonus.

Finance – Markets, Instruments & Investments

4.3 Financial Risk Measurement

We have already mentioned the rather obvious fact that an ordinary stock is riskier to hold than money in a bank account. However, how do we tell whether a certain stock is more or less risky than another stock? Or more generally, how do we quantify the risk of a financial asset whose price moves in a stochastic (random-like) fashion? This is obviously an extremely important question to answer.

In financial analysis, the *standard deviation*, σ, of an asset's price changes is the most important risk measure.[18] There are other risk measures (we will discuss a particularly important one, i.e. the β-value, in a later chapter) but none has earned a level of popularity even close to that of the standard deviation. The reason is that the standard deviation is a very intuitive measure of risk. In finance, the standard deviation of an asset's price movements is often called the asset's *volatility*. In this book we use the two terms standard deviation and volatility interchangeably.

You can think of a more volatile asset as being one with more widely fluctuating prices. In Figure 4.1, for instance, it is quite clear that the Sfax&Co. stock is more volatile than the Djem&Co. stock. Quantitatively, the standard deviation of the returns of the Sfax&Co. stock, σ_{Sfax}, is higher than the standard deviation of the returns of the Djem&Co. stock, σ_{Djem}, which is a more rigorous way of saying that buying a stock in Sfax&Co. is riskier than buying one in Djem&Co.

---

[18] The square of the standard deviation, σ, is called the variance, σ^2.

© The Author and Studentlitteratur

Finance – Markets, Instruments & Investments

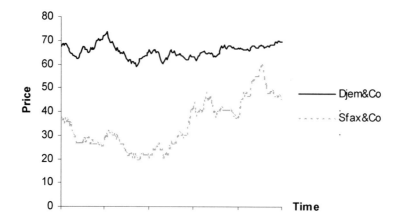

Figure 4.1 Stock prices of the two companies Djem&Co. and Sfax&Co.

Anyone who is familiar with basic statistics knows that the *standard deviation*, σ, is easy to calculate, but to do so we first need an estimate of the *mean*, μ, of the stock returns. That is, we need to estimate two parameters describing the *probability distribution* of the stock returns. The distribution here is simply the set of probabilities of all the possible returns of a particular stock. If the distribution is known, then the mean and standard deviation can easily be calculated with the following two formulas

$$\mu = E[R] = \sum_{i=1}^{n} p_i r_i \qquad (4.1)$$

and

$$\sigma = \sqrt{E\left[(R-\mu)^2\right]} = \sqrt{\sum_{i=1}^{n} p_i (r_i - \mu)^2} \qquad (4.2)$$

where p_i is the probability of the return being r_i. The n different r_i and p_i make up the stock return distribution which describes all the feasible

Finance – Markets, Instruments & Investments

returns and their associated probabilities. The expression *E*[] is short-hand for the expected value.

To better understand how it all works we will look at an example.

Example 4.3
Consider two companies, Ski-Sinistra and Ski-Destra. The returns of the two companies' stocks depend on the average weather in the Italian Alps during the year. The two stocks' possible returns over the coming year and each return's probability are summarized in the table below. The figures describe the two probability distributions of Ski-Sinistra's and Ski-Destra's stock returns.

Weather	Probability	Ski-Sinistra	Ski-Destra
Sunny	0.20	20%	40%
Cloudy	0.10	15%	10%
Snowy	0.40	0%	0%
Windy	0.20	-10%	-20%
Rainy	0.10	-5%	-10%

Since the return distributions are known, it is easy to calculate the means and standard deviations of the two stocks' returns. The mean return is often called the *expected return* and in the rest of this book we will use both terms interchangeably.[19] Using equations (4.1) and (4.2) above we get

$$\mu_{Ski-Sinistra} = 0.2 \cdot 20 + 0.1 \cdot 15 + 0.4 \cdot 0 + 0.2 \cdot (-10) + 0.1 \cdot (-5) = 3\%$$
$$\mu_{Ski-Destra} = 0.2 \cdot 40 + 0.1 \cdot 10 + 0.4 \cdot 0 + 0.2 \cdot (-20) + 0.1 \cdot (-10) = 4\%$$

and

$$\sigma_{Ski-Sinistra} = \sqrt{0.2 \cdot (20-3)^2 + 0.1 \cdot (15-3)^2 + 0.4 \cdot (0-3)^2 + 0.2 \cdot (-10-3)^2 + 0.1 \cdot (-5-3)^2} = 10.8\%$$
$$\sigma_{Ski-Destra} = \sqrt{0.2 \cdot (40-4)^2 + 0.1 \cdot (10-4)^2 + 0.4 \cdot (0-4)^2 + 0.2 \cdot (-20-4)^2 + 0.1 \cdot (-10-4)^2} = 20.1\%$$

The expected return of the Ski-Sinistra stock is lower than that of the Ski-Destra stock but at the same time the risk, measured as the standard deviation of the return distribution, is significantly lower. The risk of the Ski-Destra stock is close to double that of Ski-Sinistra's. This can also be

---

[19] The mean of the distribution can be interpreted as its center of gravity.

© *The Author and Studentlitteratur*

Finance – Markets, Instruments & Investments

seen in the two distributions where it is clear that Ski-Destra's distribution, in some sense, is "wider".

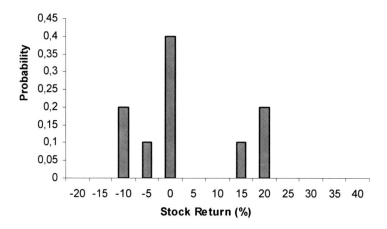

Ski-Sinistra's stock return distribution.

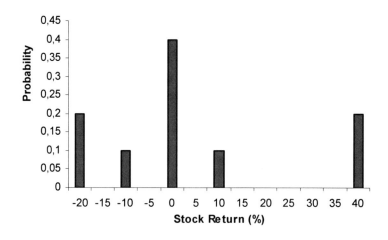

Ski-Destra's stock return distribution.

The asset return distributions you will encounter in this book are of the type described in Example 4.3, i.e. discrete, which means that there is a discrete (finite) number of possible states (such as the five states Sunny, Cloudy, Snowy, Windy and Rainy in the example). In real world situations it is more common to encounter continuous probability distributions where the observed parameter, maybe the temperature in London (UK) or the IQ of a business student in Lund (Sweden), may take on any value. These continuous distributions are often easier to work with and a machinery of analytical (mathematical) results can be relied upon. We will not discuss these distributions at any length in this book, but the *normal* distribution (sometimes also called the *Gaussian* distribution), which is the most common probability distribution, is so important that it needs to be touched on here. Two normal distributions with different means and standard deviations are shown in Figure 4.2.

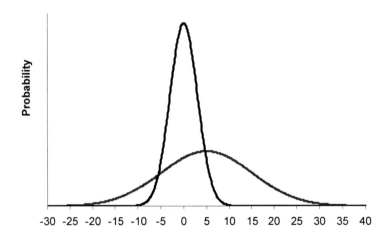

Figure 4.2 Two normal distributions, N(0,3) and N(5,10), with different means and standard deviations.

The normal distribution is always symmetric and bell-shaped. It is completely described by its mean and standard deviation, which is one of its nice features. If a financial asset (such as gold) has a return distribution that follows a normal distribution with mean μ and standard deviation σ, then it is represented, analytically, as $r_{\text{Gold}} \sim N(\mu, \sigma)$. The two distributions in Figure 4.2 can therefore be described as $N(0,3)$ and $N(5,10)$.

4.4 Financial Risk Management

The *measurement of risk* was discussed in section 4.3, and volatility was used as an example of a common measure of risk. This section deals with the *management of risk*, which usually means reduction of risk, where hedging, insuring and diversifying are examples of risk management techniques. Each of these techniques will be thoroughly discussed later in this book, so this chapter will only provide an introduction to the three important concepts:

- *Hedging: you reduce your risk by reducing your risk exposure. In essence, you pay by giving up the potential for gains. Or stated differently, you give up the upside in order to remove the downside.*

- *Insuring: you reduce your risk by paying someone to accept the risk. In essence, you buy insurance against unwanted scenarios. Or stated differently, you remove the downside but keep the upside. Obviously, you have to pay for this win-only situation.*

- *Diversifying: you reduce your risk by not putting all your eggs in the same basket. In that way the worst scenarios are avoided. Or stated differently, you spread your investments and pay for the risk reduction by giving up the really good scenarios.*

Hedging is often accomplished through buying and selling *forward* and *futures contracts*. These contract types (financial instruments) will be discussed at length in chapter 7. Basically, if you buy something, such as a ton of cacao, using a forward (or future) contract, you buy the cacao

Finance – Markets, Instruments & Investments

today for a price that is determined today but the delivery and the money transaction will take place at a certain date in the future. In this way you have *hedged* yourself against cacao price fluctuations since you know today how much the cacao will cost you in the future. This is a common way for companies to manage their financial risks and in some markets the forward market is even larger than the ordinary *spot* market.

For private individuals, an *insurance* contract is typically a deal between the individual and an insurance company. For the typical financial institution, however, insurance is often arranged with instruments that resemble financial securities rather than insurance contracts. An *option* is the classical insurance-like financial security that financial players use for insurance purposes; this asset class will be thoroughly discussed in chapter 8. The basic mechanism of an option is for the buyer to pay a fee upfront, the option premium, and in return he/she gets the *option* to buy (or sell) something, such as a ton of cacao, for a certain price at some date in the future. In this way the buyer of the option has insured him/herself against price-increases (or price-falls) without having to sacrifice possible profits from price-falls (price-increases). Also, notice the difference as well as the similarity compared with the forward contract.

Diversification, finally, is simply the strategy of following the old motto: *do not put all your eggs in the same basket*. The reason, clearly, is that if you are on your way home from the market and if you have put all your eggs in the same basket (pretend that you live in the 19th century), then you face the risk of losing all your eggs if you for some reason drop your egg basket. If you use two baskets instead, then the worst that can happen if you drop a basket is that half of your eggs will be broken (if you put half the eggs in each basket, that is). In this way you have reduced your risk (of getting home empty handed) compared with putting all your eggs in one basket.[20] The exact same situation holds in

---

[20] You can go on diversifying more and more by using more and more baskets. There is, of course, a limit to how many baskets you can carry and if you buy more than, let's say, six eggs, you probably will not be able to fully diversify

© *The Author and Studentlitteratur*

Finance – Markets, Instruments & Investments

modern investment situations. If you spread your investments rather than concentrating them, you will be less likely to lose the entire investment. The cost, in this case, is that by investing just a little in each of 10, 100 or maybe even 1000 different companies you give up the much larger profit resulting from investing all your money in the most successful firm. If your goal is to get rich quick (or die trying), you should not diversify! It is not by chance that Bill Gates (Microsoft) and Ingvar Kamprad (IKEA) are richer than equally investment savvy investors, such as the Swedish Wallenberg family, which has diversified (by buying stakes in several companies in different sectors of the economy) instead of putting all its money into one venture. To conclude, the "sissy" who diversifies will never be a new George Soros, but on the other hand, neither will he be a new Nick Leeson!

4.5 Summary

A central theme in finance is the pricing of various financial assets (instruments), and in this chapter we have discussed one of the most important principles to follow in asset pricing, the *law of one price*. This "law" states that identical assets should have identical prices, and it will be used throughout this book. The process that enforces the law of one price is called *arbitrage*. The law of one price is therefore often called the *arbitrage principle*. Another central concept in finance is the concept of risk, and in this chapter we have described the most common measure of financial risk, i.e. the *volatility* of asset price movements. Basically, the more variability an asset price demonstrates, the riskier the asset is considered. Volatility is certainly the most widely used measure of financial risk, but we will introduce another important risk measure, called the β-value, in chapter 10. We have also briefly described the

---

(i.e. put one egg in each basket). Furthermore, there is also the non-zero probability that if one basket slips out of your hand, you will be scared by the sudden event and possibly drop another basket in the process. In other words, the "basket drops" are not independent of each other. We will come back to this discussion of dependence/independence in chapters 9 and 10.

54   © *The Author and Studentlitteratur*

Finance – Markets, Instruments & Investments

main techniques of managing financial risk, i.e. hedging, insuring and diversifying. Each of these risk-reducing techniques will be treated more extensively in later chapters.

5. Bonds (Debt)

There are many different types of actively traded financial instruments in today's financial markets. Of these, one of the most basic instruments is the *bond*. We briefly discussed the basic features of bonds earlier, so we know that a bond is a clearly defined debt instrument that a company or government issues when they want to borrow money in the capital market. Of course, companies and governments may also borrow money from banks and other financial intermediaries, i.e. *ordinary bank loans*. One important difference between bonds and bank loans is that the latter, typically, are not actively traded in a market. Other than that, the basic principle is the same; if you lend someone money, or if you buy a bond issued by the same someone, in both cases you postpone consumption for a certain period of time and in return you earn interest on the money.

In this chapter we will learn how to price fundamental debt instruments, such as *zero-coupon bonds* and *coupon bonds*. This is important knowledge for any serious business or economics student, not least considering that debt is one of two fundamental ways for a company to finance its activities. The other is equity, i.e. ordinary stocks, and this source of financing will be discussed in the next chapter.

5.1 Annuities

An annuity is an important concept/structure that can be used in pricing coupon bonds and other financial instruments that promise multiple future cash flows. This book will treat an annuity as an abstract object introduced solely to better understand how the prices of common instruments such as coupon bonds are determined. If you like, however,

© The Author and Studentlitteratur

you can also think of an annuity as a basic financial instrument that can be bought and sold in the marketplace.

The holder of an annuity is promised a sequence of cash flows in the future. The first cash flow is paid in one year's time (or at any other date determined by the contract) and, after that, all the other cash flows are paid in sequence at equidistant time intervals. Moreover, all the cash flows are of equal size. The cash flow stream of a five-year annuity is illustrated in Figure 5.1.

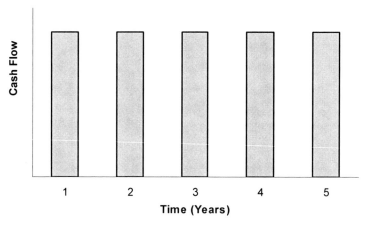

Figure 5.1 The cash flow structure of a 5-year annuity.

How do we price an annuity? Or in other words, what would an investor be willing to pay for the annuity today? To answer that question we return for a second to chapter 3 where we learned how to calculate the present value of a future cash flow. Now, since an annuity is nothing but a series of future cash flows we calculate the present value of each of these cash flows and add them up. The sum of all the present values is the price that any investor will be prepared to pay for the annuity, i.e. the market price. If the present value were higher than the market price, the buyer would make a profit since he or she would buy something for a price that is lower than its actual value. On the other hand, if it were lower, the seller would make a profit. Therefore, in a well functioning

Finance – Markets, Instruments & Investments

market one would expect buyers and sellers to agree on a price that would disappoint neither of them, i.e. the price should be equal to the present value of the cash flows.

If we assume that all interest rates, regardless of maturity, are the same, and if we apply the present value formula

$$PV = \frac{FV}{(1+r)^n} \tag{5.1}$$

to our sequence of cash flows, then we end up with the following pricing formula

$$P_{Annuity} = \frac{C}{(1+r)} + \frac{C}{(1+r)^2} + \frac{C}{(1+r)^3} + \frac{C}{(1+r)^4} + \frac{C}{(1+r)^5} \tag{5.2}$$

where r is the (risk-free) interest rate and C is the size of the cash flows.[21]

If we have an annuity with a large number of cash flows, then this way of presenting the pricing formula becomes too cumbersome and we rewrite the formula using the standard notation for a sum

$$P_{Annuity} = \sum_{i=1}^{n} \frac{C}{(1+r)^n} \tag{5.3}$$

where i is the summation index and n is the number of cash flows (the *maturity* of the annuity). On the one hand, $P_{Annuity}$ is then the price an investor is prepared to pay for the annuity. On the other hand, you can also think of $P_{Annuity}$ as the amount of money the investor has to deposit in a bank account with an interest rate r in order to be able to withdraw exactly C dollars annually the next n years.

---

[21] The interest rate has to be the risk-free one since the cash flows are known with certainty.

© *The Author and Studentlitteratur*

Finance – Markets, Instruments & Investments

Finally, with mathematics of sums[22] one can show that equation (5.3) can be rewritten as

$$P_{Annuity} = C\left(\frac{1}{r} - \frac{1}{r(1+r)^n}\right) \qquad (5.4)$$

Obviously, this is a much more convenient, and quicker, way of calculating the price of long-maturity annuities. While the price of a 25-year annuity expressed along the lines of equation (5.3) contains 25 terms that you have to type correctly into an Excel spread sheet or a pocket calculator, the price of the same 25-year annuity expressed along the lines of equation (5.4) only contains two terms. And this holds regardless of the maturity.

We end this chapter with an example of how an annuity can be priced using equations (5.3) and (5.4).

Example 5.1
What is the value of a 3-year annuity where each cash flow is $1000 and the risk-free interest rate is 5%? A straightforward application of equation (5.3) gives

$$P_{Annuity} = \frac{1000}{(1+0.05)} + \frac{1000}{(1+0.05)^2} + \frac{1000}{(1+0.05)^3} \approx \$2723$$

and an equally straightforward use of equation (5.4) gives

$$P_{Annuity} = 1000\left(\frac{1}{0.05} - \frac{1}{0.05(1+0.05)^3}\right) \approx \$2723$$

The two formulas give the same result, and the answer to the question is that in a well functioning market an investor would value this annuity at $2723.

---

[22] Again, the proof is left out of this book.

60

Finance – Markets, Instruments & Investments

5.2 Zero-Coupon Bonds

A zero-coupon bond shares many features with an ordinary savings account in a bank. In both cases you are exposed to a negative cash flow today (you buy the bond or you deposit money with the bank) and receive a positive and slightly larger cash flow at some time in the future with certainty (the bond matures or you withdraw your money from the bank account). While bonds typically mature at a certain pre-determined date, you are normally allowed to withdraw your money from a bank account at any point in time. In addition, bank account deposits cannot be bought or sold in the market, but bonds may usually be traded in the bond market. As a result, you do not *have to* wait until maturity (the bond's lifetime) to get your money back. If you prefer, you may sell the bond in the market before it matures. Obviously, in this case you usually get a smaller positive cash flow than if you wait until maturity. We will initially assume that the investor holds the bonds until maturity, which simplifies the analysis. We will then extend the analysis in section 5.4 to the situation where the investor sells the bond before it matures.

To price the zero-coupon bond we will use the same approach as the one used for pricing the annuity. In fact, pricing a zero-coupon bond is even simpler than pricing an annuity. The reason for this is that while an annuity promises the owner several future cash flows, the zero-coupon bond only promises the owner a single future payment (see Figure 5.2).

© *The Author and Studentlitteratur*

61

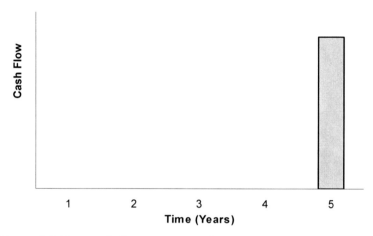

Figure 5.2 The cash flow structure of a 5-year zero-coupon bond.

As mentioned above, a zero-coupon bond offers the owner one single *certain* cash flow at a pre-defined future date. This cash flow is called the *nominal amount*, N, and the date when you are to receive the nominal amount is called n, the *maturity*. Despite its simplicity (or perhaps exactly because of its simplicity), the zero-coupon bond is an important building block in the debt world. Many other more advanced debt instruments, such as the coupon bonds in the next chapter, are built up by a set of zeroes (as they are often called).

A zero-coupon bond, being the interest-paying instrument it is, will of course always trade at a price lower than the nominal amount, N. The bond is said to trade with a *discount*. If this were not the case, then no rational investor would be prepared to buy it. For instance, no one would pay, let's say, $1100 to get $1000 in 10 years' time. In fact, no one would even pay $1000 to get $1000 in 10 years' time. Investors are only prepared to pay a sum that is smaller than $1000, and the question is just how much less the investor is prepared to pay. In other words, we have to find the market price of the bond. To do that we use the present value formula again; investors are prepared to pay the present value of the nominal amount, N, neither more nor less. Therefore, if r is the risk-free

Finance – Markets, Instruments & Investments

interest rate, you end up with the following very important pricing formula for the zero-coupon bond

$$P_{Zero} = \frac{N}{(1+r)^n} \qquad (5.5)$$

Essentially, if you pay P_{Zero} today, then you are *promised* a single future cash flow, N, in n years. Or, if you think of the zero-coupon bond as a savings account in a bank (which it obviously is not), then your deposit, which is equal to $P_{Zero,}$ will be compounding at an interest rate r for n years and after n years it will have grown to an amount equal to N.

To sum up, the zero-coupon bond is a simple and straightforward instrument (contract) and its pricing formula is therefore also simple and straightforward. Here follows an example showing how a zero-coupon bond is priced.

Example 5.2
What is the price of a 10-year zero-coupon bond issued by the German government? The nominal amount is 1 million Euro, and the risk-free interest rate is 3%. To price the bond, we use the pricing formula (5.5) as follows

$$P_{Zero} = \frac{1000000}{(1+0.03)^{10}} \approx 744000 \text{ Euro}$$

Obviously, you pay substantially less than 1 million Euro and the reason is the time value of money. At an interest rate of 3%, 1 million Euro in 10 years' time is worth 744000 Euro today.

5.3 Coupon Bonds

A coupon bond is slightly more elaborate compared to the rather simple zero-coupon bond described above. In addition to paying a nominal amount on the maturity date, the coupon bond makes periodical interest rate payments, so-called *coupons*, to the owner. Typically, the coupons are paid annually or semi-annually.

In essence, an *n*-year coupon bond is a combination of an *n*-year zero-coupon bond and an *n*-year annuity. That can be seen in Figure 5.3 where the annuity part is represented by the grey cash flows, and the zero-coupon bond part is represented by the black cash flow.

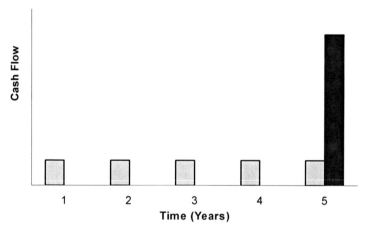

Figure 5.3 The cash flow structure of a 5-year coupon bond.

If you owned a portfolio containing an annuity and a zero-coupon bond, you would be entitled to exactly the same future cash flows as you would if you owned a coupon bond. The law of one price (see chapter 4) tells us that the portfolio and the coupon bond must be worth exactly the same. Otherwise, arbitrage opportunities would arise in the market. The price of the coupon bond is therefore equal to the sum of the annuity price and the zero-coupon bond price

$$P_{Coupon} = C\left(\frac{1}{r} - \frac{1}{r(1+r)^n}\right) + \frac{N}{(1+r)^n} \qquad (5.6)$$

Finance – Markets, Instruments & Investments

The first term in equation (5.6) comes from the annuity part and the second term comes from the zero-coupon part. Again, we assume that all interest rates are the same, regardless of maturity. In reality, one has to take into consideration the fact that interest rates at different maturities might differ. The pricing formula will then be slightly modified.

Sometimes the size of the coupon is given in relation to the nominal amount. This is called the *coupon rate, c*, i.e. the annual total coupon payment divided by the nominal amount, C/N. If a bond has a nominal amount equal to 100000 Yen and pays an annual coupon of 7000 Yen, then the coupon rate of that bond is 7%.

A coupon bond can be classified as belonging to one of three classes:

- if $P = N \Leftrightarrow$ the bond is trading at par
- if $P < N \Leftrightarrow$ the bond is trading at a discount
- if $P > N \Leftrightarrow$ the bond is trading at a premium

This classification only applies to coupon bonds since zero-coupon bonds always trade at a discount. The relationship between P and N is closely related to the relationship between the coupon rate, c, and the interest rate r; the current price of a coupon bond is lower than the nominal amount if, and only if, the coupon rate is lower than the current interest rate.

We end this section with an example of how to price a coupon bond.

Example 5.3
What is the price of a 2-year coupon bond issued by the Canadian government? The nominal amount is 1 billion CAD (Canadian dollars) and the coupon rate is 6%. The bond pays a coupon annually. The risk-free interest rate is 3%. Using the pricing formula (5.6) gives

© The Author and Studentlitteratur

$$P_{Coupon} = 60000000\left(\frac{1}{0.03} - \frac{1}{0.03(1+0.03)^2}\right) + \frac{1000000000}{(1+0.03)^2} \approx$$

$$\approx 1057400000CAD$$

Somewhat peculiarly (it seems), the buyer of the bond pays as much as 1.057 billion CAD to get a mere 1 billion CAD in 2 years' time! The reason is simply that the coupons are very large compared to today's interest rate level. That's why the buyer is prepared to pay more than the nominal amount for the bond.

5.4 Bond Prices, Time and Interest Rates

So far, we have assumed that the bondholder keeps the bond until maturity, i.e. he or she does not actively sell the bond in the marketplace. Of course, this is not necessarily true, as in real life many bonds are actively bought and sold several times during their lifetime. How is the bond price determined in these cases?

Throughout this chapter we will limit ourselves to zero-coupon bonds, and to how their prices vary when time passes and interest rates change.[23] If we look at the right-hand side of the pricing formula (5.5), there are only two things that can affect the price of a particular zero-coupon bond; the time left to maturity (which of course decreases one day for each day that passes) and the interest rate. The nominal amount, on the other hand, is fixed from the beginning.

Keeping in mind that the time to maturity of a particular bond decreases over time, after two years a 5-year bond will have three years left to maturity. Three months after that the bond will have two years and nine months left to maturity and so on. In all these situations, if we assume that the interest rate remains constant, the only thing that has changed in equation (5.5) is n. Consequently, it is completely straightforward to price a bond at any point during its life; just replace n with the current

---

[23] The analysis is similar for coupon bonds.

66   © The Author and Studentlitteratur

Finance – Markets, Instruments & Investments

time left to maturity. The price of a zero-coupon bond as a function of time is demonstrated in Figure 5.4, and, as a result of the non-linear relationship between *P* and *n* in equation (5.5), the price changes in a non-linear fashion with time.

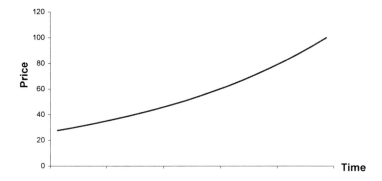

Figure 5.4 The price of a zero-coupon bond with N=100 as a function of time.

Now, let us look at Example 5.2 again:

Example 5.2*
The buyer of the German 10-year government bond in Example 5.2 now wants to sell the bond after only two years. We assume that the interest rate remains unchanged at 3%. The price of the zero-coupon bond after two years (the bond has now become an 8-year bond) is then

$$P_{Zero} = \frac{1000000}{(1+0.03)^8} \approx 789000 \text{Euro}$$

So, after two years the investor could sell the bond that he or she bought at 744000 Euro for 789000 Euro. The difference between 789000 Euro and 744000 Euro is the investor's profit, and the percentage difference is the investor's return on the investment.

In this example we have assumed that the interest rate has remained constant. In reality, of course, interest rates change from day to day. To study the effect of a change in the interest rate on the zero-coupon bond price, we simply assume that the time to maturity remains constant (we assumed above that the interest rate remained constant). In other words, on a particular day, what happens to the bond price if the interest rate suddenly changes?

This time, the only thing that has changed in equation (5.5) is the interest rate, r. If the interest rate suddenly goes up, perhaps due to an unexpected interest rate increase by the central bank, then the bond price falls. That is, an interest rate increase is bad news for the bondholder. The exact relationship is shown in Figure 5.5 and as you can see the relationship is non-linear. Again, this is of course a result of the non-linear relationship between P and r in equation (5.5).

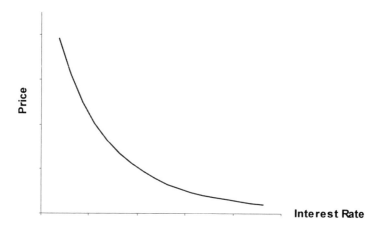

Figure 5.5 The price of a zero-coupon bond as a function of the interest rate.

Let's return to Example 5.2 for a third time:

Example 5.2**
This time, the interest rate is assumed to fall instantaneously from 3% to 2.5%. The time to maturity of the bond is still 10 years, however, and

due to the interest rate change the price of the zero-coupon bond instantaneously increases from 744000 Euro to

$$P_{Zero} = \frac{1000000}{(1+0.025)^{10}} \approx 781000 \text{ Euro}$$

Again, the difference between 781000 Euro and 744000 Euro is the profit and the percentage difference is the return. Since the interest rate has fallen, the return is positive. If the interest rate had risen instead, the return (profit) to the zero-coupon bond investor would have been negative.

Up to now we have, somewhat artificially, assumed that we can *isolate* either the time change or the interest rate change. In reality, of course, time and interest rate changes occur in tandem. We obviously cannot stop time and anyone who has watched the business news on TV knows that each day the news-anchor presents a new interest rate figure. So, in reality, both the time effect and the interest-rate effect have to be acknowledged. A typical scenario is presented in Figure 5.6. As time goes by the interest rate changes, and so does the bond price. The "jumpy" price dynamics are caused by the daily change in the interest rate.

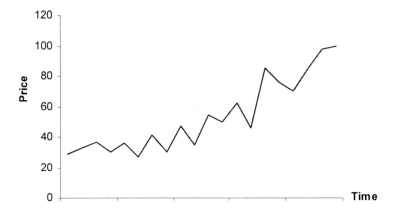

Figure 5.6 The price of a zero-coupon bond with N=100 as a function of time, allowing for interest rate changes.

Finance – Markets, Instruments & Investments

We end this chapter with a more realistic version of Example 5.2.

> Example 5.2***
> In reality, if the investor wants to sell his or her government bond after two years, the interest rate might have fallen, perhaps to 2.5%. The time to maturity of the bond has also fallen, to 8 years, and due to the combined fall in interest rate and time to maturity the price of the zero-coupon bond has increased from 744000 Euro to
>
> $$P_{Zero} = \frac{1000000}{(1+0.025)^8} \approx 821000 \text{Euro}$$
>
> Again, the difference between 821000 Euro and 744000 Euro is the profit to the investor, and this time the investor has been compensated not only for the fall in interest rate but also for the passage of time.

5.5 Government Bonds versus Corporate bonds

Not only governments issue bonds when they have borrowing needs; companies do as well. The important difference between a government bond, also called a treasury bond, and a corporate bond is that the latter exposes the investor to credit risk. This simply means that a company has a certain non-zero probability of defaulting (failing to pay back the nominal amount or coupons) on its bonds. This could be due to the company going bankrupt or to some other problem that makes it impossible for the company to pay back the debt. Governments, on the other hand, are usually assumed to have zero credit risk since they have such a low probability of defaulting on their bonds.[24] We will just briefly introduce the concept of credit risk in this chapter. A more complete discussion can be found in chapter 12, which focuses entirely on credit and credit risk.

---

[24] While bonds issued by countries such as the US or Japan bear infinitesimal credit risk, some smaller countries' bonds do indeed carry credit risk.

70   © *The Author and Studentlitteratur*

Finance – Markets, Instruments & Investments

All the bonds discussed above were assumed to be issued by a stable government with zero probability of defaulting on its bonds. As a consequence, the interest rate used to price the bonds was the risk-free interest rate. However, if we want to price a bond issued by a company, such as those issued by the German chemical company BÖCF (Badische Öl- und Chemie-Fabrik), we have to use a somewhat higher interest rate when we discount the bond's nominal amount and the coupons. The reason is of course that these cash flows no longer are 100% certain. Instead, there is a small probability that BÖCF will fail to pay back the loan, in which case we have lost our entire investment. Moreover, the larger this risk, the higher the interest rate used in the bond pricing formula.

Even though only a small modification to the pricing formulae (5.5) and (5.6) is needed in order to price credit-risky bonds, the extra risk-premium that has to be added to the risk-free interest rate is hard to estimate and needs thorough analysis. Partly as a result of this, corporate debt investment has turned into an area of its own, somewhat separate from ordinary debt investments. Sometimes this field is called *credit* (see chapter 12). Consequently, credit is now often treated as an asset class on its own, just like debt, real estate, equity or any other traditional asset class. Furthermore, the estimation and management of credit risk have become one of the fastest growing fields of finance over the last decade.

In the following example we assume that we somehow have estimated the credit risk premium required by the market to take on the credit risk of BÖCF.

Example 5.4
What is the price of a 10-year zero-coupon bond issued by the German company BÖCF? The nominal amount is 1 million Euro. As above, the risk-free interest rate is 3%, but here we also need the (credit) risk premium required by the market. We assume that this premium somehow has been estimated to be 2% (by the investor). Consequently, the price the investor is prepared to pay for the corporate bond is

© The Author and Studentlitteratur

71

Finance – Markets, Instruments & Investments

$$P_{Zero} = \frac{1000000}{\left(1+0.03+0.02\right)^{10}} \approx 614000\text{Euro}$$

The investor will pay less for the corporate bond issued by BÖCF than for the bond issued by the German government (744000 Euro) and the reason is of course the credit risk of BÖCF. There is a small probability of BÖCF going bankrupt during the lifetime of the bond (perhaps 1-10% probability) while the German government is more or less certain to survive another ten years (the maturity of the bond). What happens after that is of no interest to the investor.

5.6 Summary

In this chapter we have discussed the features of the basic debt instruments *zero-coupon bonds* and *coupon bonds*. Zero-coupon bonds are the most basic discount instruments and may be thought of as tradable (fixed interest rate) loans. Coupon bonds, in turn, may be thought of as a portfolio of zero-coupon bonds packaged within one structure. Their prices are therefore given by the sum of the individual zero-coupon bond prices. While zero-coupon bonds only pay out money at maturity, coupon bonds pay regular (annual or semi-annual) coupons. The coupons can be thought of as regular interest rate payments. The price of a bond is easy to calculate and it changes over time and with changing interest rate levels in the economy. Typically, bond prices fall when interest rates go up (perhaps due to the central bank tightening the inflation-target rate). Finally, it is important to understand that companies as well as governments can issue bonds. The main difference is that companies have to pay a higher interest rate due to their non-zero credit risk. That is, a company can go bankrupt, in which case the lender never gets the money back. Governments of major countries are usually assumed to be credit risk-free.

6. Stocks (Equity)

The concept of ordinary stocks (also called shares, risk capital or equity) issued by a stock company is completely intuitive. Basically, if you own a Toyota stock, you own a small share of Toyota, the automobile company. If there is a total of one million Toyota stocks in the market, you simply own one millionth of the firm for each stock you hold. Companies such as Toyota are called stock companies and in this chapter we are going to discuss how the stocks issued by such companies are priced.

When all the stocks of a stock company are held by one person (or family or holding company), the company is said to be a *private company* (or tightly-held company). Often, however, the ownership of a firm is widely dispersed among many small owners. Many of the companies that you have heard of, and most likely those that you have bought a share of in the stock market, are such *public companies* with stocks traded on stock exchanges.[25]

6.1 Dividends

The owner of, let's say, a tenth of the stocks in a company is also the owner of a tenth of the actual company, at least after all the debt is repaid. This also means that the stockholder has the legal right to his or her share of the company's profits. Since a significant share of the profit is typically reinvested in the company (i.e. the profit is used to finance

---

[25] This division between privately held companies and public companies should not be confused with the distinction between companies owned by governments and those owned by private investors (irrespective of whether there is one owner or thousands of owners).

© *The Author and Studentlitteratur*

Finance – Markets, Instruments & Investments

international expansions, launching new product lines, buying other companies etc.), only a fraction of the actual profit is normally distributed to the owners. This amount, which is transferred to the stockholder on an annual basis, is called the *dividend*.

Historically, the dividend has been the main compensation to the stockholder for supplying funds to the company (through his/her ownership in the company). Today, however, more and more focus has been shifted to expected capital gains. That is, the typical stockholder expects to get the majority of his wealth increase from an increase in the stock price. This is not to suggest that dividends are of less importance today. In fact, among other things, they are fundamental for the understanding of how the price of a stock is determined. This will be discussed in section 6.2.

A company that pays a higher dividend is often automatically regarded as a better company to invest in, but it is not always the case. The reason is the lack of an automatic link between the company's profit and the size of the dividend. The size of the dividend is decided by the company's board of directors and even if a healthy profit raises the potential dividend that can be paid out, the management may still choose to pay a lower dividend. One reason could be that the company is growing very fast and that the management sees a lot of interesting future investment possibilities for the company. In such a case, the profit of the company might be better used for these investments than as a dividend to the owners. Consequently, a low dividend can actually signal that a company is doing extremely well rather than the opposite. Of course, it can also be a signal of a struggling firm barely managing to pay back anything to the owners. Moreover, regardless of investment opportunities etc., remember that the more you pay out as a dividend today the less you have left to pay out next year. Such long-term considerations can also affect the size of the current dividend.

74   *© The Author and Studentlitteratur*

Finance – Markets, Instruments & Investments

6.2 Pricing Stocks

If you have ever bought a stock, you will know that stock prices fluctuate significantly over time. Sometimes you regret having bought the stock and you tend to keep quiet about your investment (if the price falls well below your purchasing price), and sometimes you are very happy to tell everyone about your excellent investment (if the price increases significantly compared to your purchasing price).

Why do stock prices fluctuate as much as they do? How do you determine what a reasonable price is? These are important questions that, unfortunately, are quite difficult to answer. For instance, if I really knew how to price stocks I would not be sitting here in my spartan office writing this book! I am certainly not the only one with these difficulties either. On the other hand, if the price of a stock was easy to find, we would not expect the high average stock returns that we have grown accustomed to. If stock prices were as predictable as, let's say, bond prices, then why should stock returns be much higher than bond returns?

There is in fact a close linkage of the three concepts (i) high returns, (ii) large price fluctuations and (iii) pricing difficulties. It is very unlikely that the three will not appear together. It may seem surprising but the uncertainty around the value of a company is one of the attractions of equity investments. Moreover, the compensation to the investor that has superior information about the company's qualities can be significant. Compared to a bond, whose future price is pretty much known, a stock's future price is highly uncertain As a result, the stock market is full of gamblers and besserwissers who all think they can outsmart the rest of us. History has shown, however, that it is easy to fool yourself into believing you are a stock-picking wizard. One has to remember always that in order to beat the market systematically (once or twice one may, of course, beat the market by pure chance), one somehow has to base one's trading on information that the market has not already incorporated in the stock price. For those of us who do not have access to such information advantages, it might simply be better to be humble and "bend for" the market.

© *The Author and Studentlitteratur*

Finance – Markets, Instruments & Investments

The discussion in the previous paragraphs might sound pessimistic and surprisingly humble for someone who has invested (reasonably success-fully) in the stock market for more than fifteen years. However, even if you feel nothing like a stock-picking wizard, there are still some simple methods/models available that may at least help you some way towards making better investments. One such model, which is widely used in the investment industry, is the *dividend discount model* (DDM).[26] Although the model might seem somewhat crude and academic initially, it is still an important step in the right direction. It is a very basic model, like a Harley-Davidson motorcycle just out of the factory, and it can be modified in any way you like (just like the Harley). It should be stressed from the outset, however, that the model suffers from some quite serious weaknesses. We will discuss this in more detail after describing the model.

The crucial idea behind the dividend discount model (DDM) is the following:

> *The price of a stock is equal to the present value of all expected future dividends.*

One might wonder why future dividends should determine the current stock price. Should today's price not be determined by tomorrow's price? Would an investor not be willing to pay more the more the stock is expected to be worth in the future? The answer is yes, obviously! The thing is, though, that the future stock price is actually hidden within the future dividend stream! Why this is so should be clear to the reader after he or she has read the following derivation of the DDM.

Let P_j be the *price* of the stock in year j and let D_j be the stock's *expected dividend per share* in year j (*today, $j = 0$*). We also have to determine the return that the market expects from this stock investment. The expected

---

[26] Sometimes the model is called the *discounted dividend model* (DDM).

76   *© The Author and Studentlitteratur*

Finance – Markets, Instruments & Investments

return is called the *market discount rate*, k, and we will explain how this discount rate can be calculated in chapter 10. For the moment we simply assume that it is known to us.

Since the expected return on the stock is the expected dividend plus the expected stock price increase (divided by the initial price to get the return in %) we have the following equation

$$\frac{D_1 + P_1 - P_0}{P_0} = k \qquad (6.1)$$

Today's price must be adjusted to satisfy equation (6.1) and if we reorganize the equation slightly we get

$$P_0 = \frac{(D_1 + P_1)}{(1 + k)} \qquad (6.2)$$

In other words, for the stock to earn an expected one-year return equal to k, today's stock price must be equal to the present value (where the discounting is done at the market rate k) of the sum of the expected dividend and the expected price next year.

The observant reader might notice a critical problem with this pricing formula; namely, to get an estimate of *today's* stock price one needs an estimate of *next year's* stock price! If there are difficulties estimating today's stock price, then there are likely to be even more difficulties estimating future stock prices. Luckily, there is an ingenious way of getting around the problem. If we just follow the scheme above, once again, but calculate an expression for P_1 instead of for P_0, we end up with the following equation

$$P_1 = \frac{(D_2 + P_2)}{(1 + k)} \qquad (6.3)$$

© *The Author and Studentlitteratur*

Finance – Markets, Instruments & Investments

And if we substitute P_1 in equation (6.2) for this expression we end up with the following expression for today's stock price

$$P_0 = \frac{\left(D_1 + \dfrac{(D_2 + P_2)}{(1+k)} \right)}{(1+k)} = \frac{D_1}{(1+k)} + \frac{(D_2 + P_2)}{(1+k)^2} \qquad (6.4)$$

If we repeat this an infinitive number of times we get

$$P_0 = \frac{D_1}{(1+k)} + \frac{D_2}{(1+k)^2} + \frac{D_3}{(1+k)^3} + \dots = \sum_{t=1}^{\infty} \frac{D_t}{(1+k)^t} \qquad (6.5)$$

We are now back to where we started: *today's stock price is equal to the present value of all the future expected dividends, discounted with the market discount rate!* And as we have seen (equation (6.1)), the future stock price is indeed incorporated, albeit implicitly, in this somewhat odd-looking pricing formula.[27]

In theory, at least, the general DDM is a very appealing model. In reality, however, it has at least one serious practical problem; in order to price the stock we need to estimate an *infinite* number of future dividends![28] To solve this problem we make one more assumption; we simply assume that the dividends grow at a certain constant growth rate, *g*. This simplifies the problem significantly since if the dividend grows at a constant rate

---

[27] P_∞, i.e. the price of the stock into the infinite future drops out of the equation since its present value is infinitely small.

[28] In practical situations it is often sufficient to estimate, let's say, 10-15 future dividends. After including 15 terms or so in the summation, each additional term adds very little to the sum (i.e., to the price) since the present value keeps getting smaller the further into the future we move. Still, estimating the 15 dividends that are expected in the 15 years to come is no easy task either.

78 © *The Author and Studentlitteratur*

Finance – Markets, Instruments & Investments

$$D_t = D_1(1+g)^{t-1} \tag{6.6}$$

and if we substitute D_t in equation (6.5) with the expression in equation (6.6), we end up with[29]

$$P_0 = \frac{D_1}{k-g} \tag{6.7}$$

Now we only need to estimate one future dividend, i.e. next year's, plus the dividend growth rate. The model resulting in equation (6.7) is called the *constant growth rate* DDM.

Still, it is not completely straightforward to apply this simple model in real-life situations, the reason being that, while conceptually simple, estimating next year's dividend in real-life situations is far from easy. We will not discuss this problem here, however. The interested reader is referred to more advanced books on stock valuation.

We end this chapter with an example.

Example 6.1
The previously privately-held Russian firm Kalas-Nikov has issued stocks and is now a publicly traded stock company. We want to price a Kalas-Nikov stock and we have decided to use the *constant growth rate* DDM. The dividend growth rate is estimated to be 2%, and the market discount rate is computed (using tools from chapter 10) to be 7%. Then, we estimate next year's dividend to 5 Ruble. Thus, today's Kalas-Nikov stock price, P_{today}, is estimated to be

---

[29] We have deliberately left out some steps here. Essentially, we go from equation (6.5) to equation (6.7) by using well known results from the theory of mathematical series and sums. As this is not a mathematics book, we skip these steps.

© *The Author and Studentlitteratur*

79

$$P_{Today} = \frac{D_1}{k-g} = \frac{5}{0.07-0.02} = 100 \text{Ruble}$$

If the Kalas-Nikov stock's market price on the Russian stock exchange happens to be 75 Ruble, we might be able to strike a good deal by buying Kalas-Nikov stocks for 75 Ruble when they are really worth 100 Ruble (if our model and model assumptions are correct, that is).

6.3 Stock Prices and Psychology – The Beauty Contest

Some people do not believe that using models such as the one described above is the best way of deciding whether to buy or sell a stock. John Maynard Keynes, the great British Economist of the early 20th century, was one of them. According to Keynes, investors would be better off applying psychological principles than financial valuation principles when making stock investment decisions. Keynes argued that *a stock (or any other security) is worth only as much as someone else is prepared to pay for it*! Therefore, as a cunning investor you should not think that much about what *you* think the stock is worth, but rather about what you think *the average investor* thinks it is worth. In fact, the logic goes one step further and Keynes likened it to a beauty contest.

The logic goes as follows. Let's pretend that you take part in a contest where you have to pick the winner in a beauty pageant. The winner receives a prize, in addition to the awe of the rest of the crowd, for spotting true beauty. As Keynes realized, you not only have to decide on who you think is the most beautiful, but also take into consideration what the others think. Besides, you also have to take into account the fact that they will probably behave just like you (and try to assess what other people think about what other people think and so on). In other words, you have to predict what the average opinion is likely to be about the average opinion etc.... over and over again. So, in fact, the winner of the beauty-picking contest is not the one who has an eye for true beauty, but rather the one who has a feeling for what other people think other

Finance – Markets, Instruments & Investments

people consider other people think beauty is! True beauty might perhaps not be in the eyes of the beholder, after all!

If we return to the world of investments, this way of thinking may also be applied to stock picking. In fact, it is the argument behind Keynes' approach to stock investments. His investment ideas were that you should look as much at the future behavior of the average investor as at trying to estimate the true intrinsic value of the stock.[30]

Even today, this psychological School attracts a significant share of followers; its study of the psychological behavior of investors is sometimes called *behavioral finance*. The same psychological behavior of the investors also forms the underpinnings of a stock-picking methodology called *technical analysis*. This, often derided, stock-picking approach is not to be dismissed as nonsense and we will therefore turn to a brief comparison of technical analysis and the fundamental analysis underlying the use of models such as the dividend discount model (DDM).

6.4 Fundamental Analysis versus Technical Analysis

Most skilled investors take into consideration not only what they believe are the fundamentals behind a firm's success but also what other people think of the firm. Despite this, however, one often divides investors into two groups, those who rely on *fundamental analysis* and those who rely on *technical analysis*.

Fundamental analysis relies on the market being inefficient in the sense that information relevant for the stock is not already incorporated in its market price.[31] In other words, by exploiting your "secret" piece of

---

[30] Whether this strategy was also the secret behind Keynes phenomenal investment record in the 1930s and 1940s I leave for others to comment upon.

[31] A stock market is said to be inefficient if there is freely available information that is not yet reflected in the stock price. Or put differently, if new positive

© The Author and Studentlitteratur

Finance – Markets, Instruments & Investments

information you could make a profit from buying or selling stocks. For instance, if you had realized earlier than anyone else that the Chinese thirst for metals and other commodities in Africa would increase the need for banking services in Africa, you would have bought shares in the Dutch bank ONG Bank (a bank that is very active in Africa and in other emerging markets) because you would have expected it to continue being one of the first banks entering virgin grounds. Of course, the "secret" is not *given* to you but rather *acquired* by you through intelligent use of the available information. The process of predicting the price of a stock using all the possible relevant information that you can get hold of is called fundamental analysis since it focuses on the fundamental value of the firm. In the African example, the fundamental analyst thinks the value of ONG Bank will rise in the future because of its potential to reap profits from providing financial services to an expanding African economy.

Technical analysis, on the other hand, relies on the market being inefficient in the sense that past price movements alone may be used to predict future price movements (see chapter 11 for more discussion on technical analysis and the predictability of asset prices). This is quite a bold assumption. Remember, there are close to infinitely many sources of information about a firm (such as newspaper articles, yearly reports, investment bank research, gossip etc.) and you discard all but one of them (the historical chart of stock prices). In essence, technical analysts claim that they can beat the market by locking themselves into a dark room with nothing but a computer that feeds them continuously updated historical stock price charts. No wonder some people think technical analysts, or *chartists* as they are sometimes called, are a crazy bunch! Having said that, however, there seem to be investors that are able to make more than a decent living from technical analysis. Further, I do not think I am alone in secretly wishing it was possible to beat the fundamental analysts using nothing but the stock price history and

---

information regarding a certain company is released, one would expect the company's stock price to increase. If not, the market is said to be inefficient. We will discuss the efficiency of markets extensively in chapter 11.

82   *© The Author and Studentlitteratur*

Finance – Markets, Instruments & Investments

intelligent tools for technical analysis. If it were possible, one could conduct technical analysis on stocks (or on any other traded asset class) with a computer hooked up to the internet under a palm tree watching the Caribbean sunrise, instead of in the early morning hours in a cramped office on lower Manhattan. I am sure that many chartists believe that the "fundamentalists" in their small cubicles on Wall Street are the crazy ones!

To conclude, there does not seem to be a consensus on whether either technical analysis or fundamental analysis actually works. Perhaps it is best to do a little of each. And always remember to keep an eye on the psychology of the market.

6.5 Summary

Stocks are among the most widely known (and owned) financial instruments and in this chapter we have discussed their basic function as well as the basic pricing methods. If you own a stock (share) in a stock company, then you are a part owner of that company; after the company has paid off any debt it might have, the residual value goes to the stockholders. A very important property of ordinary stocks, however, is that the stockholder has *limited liability*, which simply means that the stockholder's maximum loss is equal to the initial investment. Even if the company files for bankruptcy, the loss to the stockholder never exceeds his or her initial investment. Another important feature of stocks is that they pay regular dividends to their owner. The dividend is simply a cash-payment to the stockholder, and the size of the dividend depends on many things, for example the profit of the firm. In some cases no dividend is paid out (for instance if the firm is making losses). The uncertainty of the size of the future dividend payments makes it much more difficult to price stocks than bonds (where the future payments are known in advance). Consequently, stock prices fluctuate a lot and stock price predictions are notoriously difficult to make. Even for the so-called experts! Among all the more fundamental factors determining the stock price, market psychology is an important factor that cannot be ignored.

© The Author and Studentlitteratur

7. Forwards and Futures

We will encounter our first *derivatives contracts* (*derivatives*) in this chapter. Derivatives are financial securities (contracts) whose value depends on the value of some other underlying asset. The *underlying asset* can be anything from ordinary financial assets such as stocks and bonds to more complicated "assets" such as the price of fresh salmon, the number of bankruptcies in a certain market sector, or the amount of rainfall in a certain geographical area.

There has been no limit to the imagination of derivatives traders in inventing new types of derivatives over the last three decades. Over these 30 years or so the use of derivatives has exploded and, today, the derivatives market makes up a large share of the total traded volume of financial securities. Twenty years ago, ordinary business (or economics) students could manage without basic skills in derivatives and derivatives pricing, but today the situation is completely different. A rudimentary understanding of the role and function of derivatives is important for anyone wanting to make a serious career in finance nowadays (or in business more generally for that matter). Our hope is that this chapter, together with chapter 8, will give the reader a basic understanding of two of the most important derivatives markets, the *forward* (*futures*) market and the *options* market.

7.1 Forwards and Futures – The Basics

If you pay for a bar of chocolate in the convenience store around the corner you usually expect to get the chocolate bar in your hand immediately. You do not expect the chocolate bar to be delivered in 3

Finance – Markets, Instruments & Investments

months' time. In the financial world, however, it is very common to purchase assets today for delivery tomorrow (or at some other future date). One is said to have bought the asset in the *forward* (*futures*) market.[32] Of course, financial actors equally often expect immediate delivery of the asset, just like you with the chocolate bar, and these actors are then said to have bought the asset in the *spot* market.

The forward contract is the most basic derivatives contract there is. If you enter into a forward contract, you are *obliged* to buy or sell something in the future. You do *not* have the *option* to turn the deal down.[33] Moreover, in each forward contract there is a counterparty with an identical, but opposite, exposure to yours. If *you* have the right and obligation to *buy* a ton of aluminum in July next year (you are *long* the forward contract), then *the counterparty* has the right and obligation to *sell* a ton of aluminum in July next year (he/she is *short* the forward contract). The price at which you and the counterparty will exchange the asset in the future is called the *forward price,* and the particular date of delivery is called the *maturity* date. Importantly, there is no cost associated with entering a forward contract; i.e. neither of the two counterparties pays the other one anything at the date of entering the contract (today).[34] Instead, the two parties agree on a forward price to be paid in the future (at delivery). In section 7.3 we will look into how this forward price is related to the corresponding spot price, using the *law of one price* to find the correct price.

Before we look at the role of forwards as hedging tools, we should highlight the distinction between forwards and futures. In theory, there is

---

[32] The practical differences between forwards and futures will be discussed below. Conceptually, though, the two contract types are identical and from here on, if nothing else is explicitly mentioned, I will use the term "forwards" as a substitute for "forwards and futures".

[33] Options will be treated in chapter 8.

[34] This is very different from the situation in the options market where the buyer of the options contract pays the seller for the option to buy or sell something in the future. This price is called the option premium.

86   *© The Author and Studentlitteratur*

Finance – Markets, Instruments & Investments

no fundamental difference between the two contract types. Both contracts allow the two counterparties in the forward deal to agree on the details of a future transaction today. The differences that still exist, however, are in the institutional setup of the two markets. Basically, you can think of forwards as tailor-made contracts and futures contracts as standardized contracts.[35] More exactly, the differences can be summarized as follows:

Forwards
– Forwards are *non-standardized* (tailor-made) contracts between two parties. Each forward contract has its own contractual specifications.

– Forwards are traded *over-the-counter.* That is, they are not traded on organized exchanges. Instead, the deals are struck directly between the two counterparties (over the phone).

– The underlying asset is typically *delivered* at the maturity date. At first, this might seem obvious. After all, if you buy a ton of corn in the forward market you expect the counterparty to deliver the corn to you at maturity. However, as we will se in the case of futures below, delivery is not actually necessary.

– Forward contract holders face the *credit risk* of the counterparty. There is no organized market place, or exchange, between the two counterparties and if one of the counterparties goes bankrupt before the maturity date, the forward contract is left hanging in the air.

Futures
– Futures are *standardized* contracts between two counterparties. Since they are standardized the details of the futures contract, regarding quality and quantity of the underlying asset for example, cannot take

---

[35] The difference between the two is similar to the difference between a tailor-made suit on *Savile Row* (or *Khao San Road*) and a prêt-à-porter suit in your local *Armani* store. As anyone who has bought both a tailor-made suit and a readymade one knows, they both have their pros and cons. Both are suits though.

© The Author and Studentlitteratur

on any possible value. Instead, the contractual particularities are limited to a certain set of feasible values. In the case of gold, *qualities* of 14, 18 or 24 karat and *quantities* in multiples of ten ounces could, for instance, be the only gold assets bought/sold in the futures market.

– Futures contracts are traded on organized *futures exchanges*, such as *Euronext.liffe* and *Eurex*. These exchanges are important institutions for risk managers as well as speculators and trading volumes are typically very large.

– The underlying asset is typically *not* delivered at maturity, but settled in cash. This is called *cash settlement,* which is convenient when the underlying asset is difficult or expensive to deliver (think of wheat and other commodities). The cash amount that actually changes hands is determined by a comparison of the actual spot price at the delivery date with the (fixed) future price in the contract. If the futures price of the asset is lower than the actual spot price, the buyer of the futures contract (the counterparty that is long the future) is paid the difference by the other counterparty. The buyer can then turn to the local spot market to actually buy the asset, using the surplus from the futures deal in addition to the stipulated futures price in the deal to buy the asset. Regardless of the actual spot price at the delivery date, the total net outlay for the buyer is fixed at the price in the futures contract.

– Due to the standardization, futures markets are typically more *liquid* than forward markets. With a few standardized contracts all trade is concentrated to these deals rather than to several tailor-made deals. This makes the market more liquid.

– Futures markets are organized in a way that reduces the credit risk of the two counterparties. The trading is done through an exchange, and the exchange organizes a *margin requirement* mechanism that enables contracts to be written without credit risk. Each counterparty is required to post a collateral, the *margin*, at the exchange and each day

Finance – Markets, Instruments & Investments

of the futures contract's lifetime (its maturity) the futures price in the contract is compared to the actual spot price in the market and any profits/losses incurred by the counterparties are settled by transferring funds from one margin to the other.[36] This operation is called *mark-to-market*. When (if) one of the two counterparties' margins is emptied, the counterparty has to post additional collateral or cancel the contract (in which case the other counterparty is assigned a new counterparty by the exchange and thereafter business continues as usual). When requiring additional margin in this way the exchange is said to make a *margin call*. The credit risk is thus eliminated by means of the margin mechanism.

7.2 Forwards and Futures – Risk Management Tools

Despite the fact that they are convenient tools for speculation (see section 7.4), forwards and futures are mainly used in risk management. Forwards and futures are ideal hedging tools and, through an example, we will try to describe the risk reduction mechanism behind these contracts. The distinction between forwards and futures will also be highlighted.

Imagine two Brazilian entrepreneurs, a chocolate manufacturer and a cacao grower, both of whom are exposed to fluctuations of the cacao price. The chocolate manufacturer is exposed to the risk of too high future cacao prices and the cacao grower is exposed to the risk of the cacao price falling in the future. If we assume that the cacao user needs cacao in six months' time and that the cacao producer is due to harvest the cacao at the same time, then both will profit from entering a *forward* contract with the other party. The maturity of the forward contract should be six months and the exact details regarding quantity and quality

---

[36] The mechanism of the daily mark-to-market will be better understood after reading section 7.3 where we explain how the forward price depends on the spot price.

© The Author and Studentlitteratur

Finance – Markets, Instruments & Investments

have to be determined by the two parties. In this example we simply assume that the quantity is five tons and that the cacao type is Forastero. In other words, the forward contract stipulates that the chocolate producer has the right and obligation to buy five tons of Forastero cacao from the cacao producer in six months' time. The cacao will have to be delivered by the cacao producer and since the two counterparties live in the same neighborhood we assume that the transport cost is zero. What remains to be settled before the contract can be written is the forward price, i.e. the price of the cacao in six months' time (the price of this particular batch of cacao). Here, we assume that the two forward contract counterparties agree on R$1 (Brazilian real) per kilo, i.e. R$5000 for the entire lot.

The cacao producer is said to have gone short in the forward market and the chocolate manufacturer is said to have gone long in the forward market. Both parties have done this to hedge their price risk for the next six months. Neither the cacao producer nor the chocolate producer is exposed to the daily fluctuations of the cacao price any longer and both have accomplished what they have aimed for; a reduction of their price risk. Nonetheless, as has been stressed many times before, risk reduction is usually not for free, and in this example the cost is simply the loss of the possibility of profiting from a falling (rising) cacao price for the chocolate producer (cacao grower). This is the typical situation for anyone hedging his or her risk exposure by using forwards.

What if there are no cacao growers in the neighborhood of the chocolate producer? Or, at least there is no one that the chocolate producer trusts enough to enter into a forward contract with. Or, what if the chocolate producer lives in Norway, where cacao cannot be grown?[37] Of course, the chocolate manufacturer is still exposed to the fluctuations of the world market price for cacao, but in this case it is not easy to find a counterparty with whom he/she can enter a forward contract. Instead, the cacao buyer has to turn to the *futures* market to hedge his/her risk

---

[37] Cacao can only be grown fairly close to the equator.

90   © *The Author and Studentlitteratur*

Finance – Markets, Instruments & Investments

exposure. Luckily, cacao futures are traded on futures exchanges (such as the New York Board of Trade (NYBOT)) and Brazilian as well as Norwegian cacao traders can take positions in this market. If the chocolate producer buys cacao futures on the NYBOT (goes long a futures contract) at the same time as he/she buys the actual (physical) cacao in the local cacao market, he/she is hedged in exactly the same way as entering into a forward contract with his/her neighbor. As long as the actual cacao price in the local market follows the spot cacao price in the world market, any price movements in the local market (where the actual cacao is bought) will be exactly offset by price movements in the futures market. Any losses to the cacao buyer incurred by an increased spot price are offset by identical gains from the futures contract (whose value increases in tandem with the spot price as we will see in section 7.3). The exact opposite holds for the cacao grower who hedges his/her risk exposure by selling futures. So, by organizing standardized futures exchanges, the cacao community may hedge its price risk without having to find a trustworthy counterparty on its own. The futures exchange does the search and credit risk management.

7.3 Forward (Futures) Pricing

In the previous section we saw how forwards (and futures) could be used to manage financial risk. By buying or selling an asset in the forward market, the trader knows in advance what he/she will pay/receive for the asset in the future. Up to now, however, this price, i.e. the forward price, has been given to us by divine intervention. There has been no discussion around how the market participants decide on the forward price. In reality, though, the forward price of an asset is forced by the law of one price to take on a specific value. We will now see why that is a necessity, at least in well functioning arbitrage free markets, and what the actual forward price is.

Oil traders buy and sell crude oil for their living and, like most traders, they hope to buy when it is cheap and sell when it is expensive. Now, imagine being such an oil trader. Since crude oil is such a common asset,

© The Author and Studentlitteratur

Finance – Markets, Instruments & Investments

you have the opportunity to trade crude oil using forward contracts (over-the-counter) as well as futures contracts (on futures exchanges). In addition, of course, you can also buy oil in the spot market (the usual way). The oil price in the spot market is usually not the same as that in the forward market, and in what follows we will show how the law of one price can be applied to find the one and only reasonable forward price of crude oil. In a sense, we will force the forward price to take on its correct value.[38] If you wish to buy one barrel of crude oil in the market with the aim of selling it again in one year's time, you can do so in one of two ways:

Alternative 1: Buy the oil in the spot market today, for S_0, warehouse it for one year at a warehousing cost of w (measured as a percentage of the initial oil investment, S_0), and sell it in one year's time for S_1. The return on this investment is of course equal to

$$r_{\text{Alternative 1}} = \frac{S_1 - S_0}{S_0} - w \qquad (7.1)$$

Alternative 2: Again, invest the same amount, S_0, but this time invest it in a one-year risk-free government bond paying a risk–free interest rate of r_f. In addition, you buy the oil in the forward market, i.e. you agree to buy one barrel of oil in one year's time for the forward price, F. Finally, in one year's time you sell the oil in the spot market for S_1. The return on this investment is equal to

$$r_{\text{Alternative 2}} = \frac{S_1 - F}{S_0} + r_f \qquad (7.2)$$

---

[38] Of course, the choice of oil is purely ad hoc and most other assets could be treated in the same way. It should be mentioned, though, that, in theory, the price we derive only holds for forwards, not for futures. However, for us, the small difference is negligible, and we use the forward pricing formula for futures as well without making too much of an error.

Finance – Markets, Instruments & Investments

In both alternatives you invest S_0 today (i.e. you experience a negative cash flow equal to S_0) and own one barrel of oil in one year's time with certainty. Furthermore, in both cases you sell the oil in one year's time for S_1 (i.e. you experience a positive cash flow equal to S_1). In other words, despite their different appearances, the two investment strategies are in fact identical, and as a consequence have to offer the same return to the investor, i.e. $r_{\text{Alternative 1}} = r_{\text{Alternative 2}}$. If this was not the case the market would not be free of arbitrage; an arbitrageur could simply buy oil using one of the two strategies (the cheaper), sell it using the other strategy (the more expensive) and make a return larger than r_f despite taking on zero risk.

If we follow the reasoning above and set equation (7.1) equal to equation (7.2) we get the following equality that has to hold to avoid arbitrage possibilities

$$\frac{S_1 - S_0}{S_0} - w = \frac{S_1 - F}{S_0} + r_f \tag{7.3}$$

And if we solve for F in equation (7.3) we end up with the following expression

$$F = \left(1 + r_f + w\right) \cdot S_0 \tag{7.4}$$

That is, we have an expression for the forward price in terms of the spot price. Furthermore, and as can be seen in equation (7.4), the forward price is an increasing function of the spot price; if the spot price goes up from one day to the next, so does the forward price.

This dependency of the derivative price on its underlying asset is what has given derivatives their name; their prices are *derived* from the prices of their underlying assets. Moreover, it is important to interpret the relationship in equation (7.4) as a two-way relationship, not as a one-way causality; the spot price determines the forward price but at the

© *The Author and Studentlitteratur*

Finance – Markets, Instruments & Investments

same time the forward price determines the spot price. It is an arbitrage relationship, not just a pricing formula.

If you buy oil today in the forward market the price is F, and if you buy oil today in the spot market you pay a different price, S_0. Why is that? The short and concise answer is simply: otherwise there would be arbitrage possibilities. Some of you might not feel entirely convinced by this and would like a more elaborate answer. In fact, there is an important difference between owning oil and owning the right and obligation to buy oil in the future; in Alternative 1 you have to *pay* a storage cost w on your investment, while in Alternative 2 you *receive* interest, r_f, on your investment. If the sum of the foregone interest rate and the storage cost is large, the investor is then prepared to pay much more for oil in the forward market than in the spot market. This fact determines the forward price and leads to the pricing formula in (7.4).

The relationship derived above holds for all assets that are costly to store, such as wheat, cotton, silver etc. But many financial assets cost nothing (or almost nothing) to store. An example is the ordinary stock of a stock company, and in this case the pricing formula is even simpler than that in equation (7.4) since w is equal to zero. At the same time, however, we know that stocks pay dividends. By treating the expected dividend essentially as a negative storage cost, we can use a slightly modified version of equation (7.4) to price stock forwards. There are many ways for the expected dividend, paid by the stock during the lifetime of the forward contract, to be introduced in equation (7.4), but a full description is beyond the scope of this book.

7.4 Forwards and Futures – Predictors of Spot Prices?

Up to now we have only mentioned the risk-reducing property of futures. Forwards and futures are also used for speculation; in many forward deals, done for hedging purposes, the counterparty of the forward contract is a speculator. Therefore, speculators contribute to making the

Finance – Markets, Instruments & Investments

forward market more efficient. Compared to the more obvious strategy of taking a position in the spot market, speculators can profit from taking the same position in the futures market instead. The reason is simple; you do not have to pay anything (or just a small amount) upfront! If you buy 1000 barrels of oil in the spot market, you will have to come up with around $60000 to close the deal (if the crude oil price is $60 a barrel). However, if you buy 1000 barrels of oil in the futures market, you only have to post the margin with the futures exchange. If the margin is 20%, you only have to invest $12000, which is a huge difference. Of course, at the same time the risk is higher if you invest your money in the futures market compared to investing the same amount of money in the spot market. With a 20% margin the oil price only has to fall 20% to completely wipe out your investment. If you invested your money in the spot market instead, only one fifth of your money would be lost. Obviously, the opposite holds if the oil price goes up and that is one of the attractions of the forward (and futures) market.

As a speculator you are likely to make predictions about the future spot price and take positions accordingly in order to profit from the perceived price increase or fall. In this context, however, one of the most common misconceptions is that the forward price is an unbiased forecast of the future spot price. The mistake is understandable; after all, it sounds quite natural to expect that the six-month oil future price quoted in your daily business newspaper is the market's expectation of the spot price of oil in six months' time. Unfortunately, (for the speculator) this is not the case. John Maynard Keynes looked into the relationship between spot and forward prices as far back as the 1930s and one of his conclusions was that if speculators on average hold long forward positions, and hedgers therefore on average hold short forward positions, then $F < E[S_t]$.[39] The reason is that speculators are only attracted to the forward market if they are compensated for the risk with an expected increase in the price of the forward they have bought. Hedgers, on the other hand, are happy to enter a contract with a negative return since they are prepared to pay for their

---

[39] $E[S_t]$ means today's *expectation* of the future *spot price*.

© *The Author and Studentlitteratur*

Finance – Markets, Instruments & Investments

risk reduction. If the situation is the opposite, i.e. if speculators on average hold a short position in the forward market, then $F > E[S_l]$ must hold for speculators to be prepared to short the asset. The situation when $F < E[S_l]$ is called *normal backwardation* and the situation when $F > E[S_l]$ is called *contango*.

In other words, whether the forward price is higher or lower than the spot price depends on how speculators and hedgers in the two markets behave. This, in turn, depends on whether the systematic risk (also-called non-diversifiable risk or market risk, see chapter 10) of the asset is positive or not. If the systematic risk is positive (a positive β, see chapter 10) then $F < E[S_l]$ and if the systematic risk is negative (a negative β) then $F > E[S_l]$. Consequently, the situation in a particular market depends on the nature of the asset. Finally, only when the systematic risk of the asset is zero is $F = E[S_l]$. Speculators beware!

7.5 Summary

In this chapter we encountered our first two *derivatives*; the forward and the futures contracts. If you enter into either of these two contracts, then you have the right *and* obligation to buy or sell a particular underlying asset from or to the counterparty at a particular future date. Due to this price-fixing property of forwards and futures, they are both widely used for risk management purposes. In addition, they can also be used for speculative purposes. Futures differ from forwards only in practical matters and both are easily priced using arbitrage arguments. Basically, in an arbitrage-free market the forward (future) price differs from the spot price only by the so-called *cost of carry* (interest rate plus storage cost). This immediately tells us that the forward (future) price, in general, cannot be an unbiased forecast of the future spot price.

96   *© The Author and Studentlitteratur*

8. Options

Insurance was listed as one of three basic risk management techniques in chapter 4. If you buy insurance against a certain event, you simply pay a fee to remove the risk of the event possibly affecting you. Typical types of insurance contracts for private individuals are car-insurance, property-insurance and health-insurance contracts, all of which are not usually possible to actively buy and sell in the market place. For banks and other financial firms, however, the concept of insurance has become more or less commoditized. While a typical health-insurance contract cannot be sold to someone else if you decide that you do not want it anymore, insurance contracts in the financial world are often tradable, i.e. you can buy and sell them in the market. In this context, the typical example of an insurance contract is the *options contract*.

Options are derivatives contracts just like *forwards* (*futures*) but instead of forcing you to buy or sell something in the future at a predetermined price, options give you the *option* to buy or sell something in the future at some predetermined price. Since you have the option, and not the contractual obligation, to buy or sell something, you are left with all the upside of your investment while all the downside is removed. This property gives it a positive value (it is not for free), and it is this optionality that gives the options contract its insurance character.

A deep understanding of the exact workings of options is essential knowledge for traders and analysts working in the modern financial world. For the rest of us, it is at least necessary to grasp the basics of this extremely important component of the financial system. Our hope is that this chapter will help the reader gain this basic knowledge.

© The Author and Studentlitteratur

8.1 Some Background

Today, the derivatives markets, whether we are talking about forwards, futures, options or other more advanced derivatives, are important markets with large volumes of trade. Sometimes, the derivatives markets even dominate the underlying asset markets in terms of size. While it all started out on a small scale for a small set of underlying assets in the most advanced economies in the world, derivatives can be found on all kinds of assets in economies all over the world nowadays. In fact, the story of how the financial derivatives market has developed is a true success story.

The (modern) history of derivatives started in 19th century US and Europe when new agricultural techniques, coupled with better transportation and a significant population growth, transformed the market for agricultural products. The agricultural markets quickly changed their character from local to regional or country-wide markets. The demand and supply were no longer determined by local actors, and this made prices harder to predict. Meanwhile, larger quantities of commodities such as corn and wheat had to be stored, or kept in transport, for extended periods of time and this created a new source of price uncertainty for producers, buyers and dealers. Of course, speculators were prepared to take the risk in return for compensation, but only if legal rules and regulations were in place. The market participants had to trust that contracts would be honored, which led to the development of organized derivatives markets where speculators and hedgers could take appropriate positions.

Back in the agricultural 19th century, the derivatives were, not surprisingly, introduced in the commodities markets. Even today, commodities are very important underlying assets in derivatives markets. The most impressive growth in the use of derivatives over the last decades, however, has been in purely financial markets such as the currency, bond and stock markets.

Finance – Markets, Instruments & Investments

What has been the main driving force behind the quick development of the derivatives markets? If we are talking about the last 30-40 years, there is not one single reason behind the explosive growth rate but rather several related reasons that seem to have interacted to create today's conditions:

- First, the general *uncertainty* and increased market volatility following in the footsteps of the oil shocks in the 1970s created an increased need for insurance and hedging tools. The long periods of high (and volatile) inflation that followed the oil crises further fuelled this demand. Finally, the unprecedented speed with which the world economy has turned global (the globalization) has continued to increase uncertainty and volatility as well as the demand for risk management tools.

- Second, the *technological development* has made it possible to price, trade and settle deals in the financial markets much quicker and more efficiently than before. Think about the development in computer processing capabilities and telecommunication technologies. Furthermore, not only the technological advances, but also the *institutional developments,* have been important in speeding up the development of high-quality derivatives markets. Global deregulation, coupled with increased competition, has spurred the development of new recipes for success in the risk management business.

- Third, the development of techniques and *models for risk analysis and asset pricing* has been crucial for well-functioning derivatives markets. If it were not for pricing models such as the Black-Scholes model, the trading volumes would not even be close to the levels seen today.

Basically, it seems as if investors have been convinced that derivatives work, and this, together with the huge demand for risk management solutions, probably lies behind the fast development of the derivatives market. Moreover, the particularly fast growth of derivatives written on

Finance – Markets, Instruments & Investments

purely financial assets is most likely a result of the speed at which financial markets, at large, have grown in a more global and deregulated world. Considering the continuing speed at which the world financial markets are becoming intertwined, plus the continuing dispersion of knowledge in the field (yourself included), it is quite likely that the development in the derivatives corner of the financial system will continue in a fast-forward fashion.

8.2 Options and Forwards – Similar but Different

In the previous chapter we learned that derivatives markets, in general, have grown at an astonishing pace over the last thirty years. This also holds, more particularly, for options. The options contract is one of the most important derivatives contracts and we will focus on this contract in the rest of this chapter.

The first and foremost observation to be made is that options and forwards, however similar they at first might seem, are actually completely different contract types. Thus, we cannot expect the theory from chapter 7 to hold with only a slight modification. The two contract types can be defined succinctly in the following way

- *A forward contract gives the buyer (seller) the **right and obligation** to buy (sell) a certain underlying asset at some future date (the maturity date) for a certain predetermined price (the forward price).*

- *An options contract, on the other hand, gives the buyer the **right** to buy (or sell) a certain underlying asset at some future date (the maturity date) for a certain predetermined price (the exercise price). The seller of the option, however, has the obligation to sell (or buy) the underlying asset if the buyer of the option decides to exercise the option.*

100   *© The Author and Studentlitteratur*

Finance – Markets, Instruments & Investments

Of course, anyone in his right mind would prefer the option to the forward since the option provides everything the forward contract does except for the obligation to exercise the contract. In fact, the investor who goes long a forward contract does not usually pay anything to the short investor up front, but the buyer of the option always has to pay for the option. The fee is called the *option premium* and one of the major breakthroughs in finance theory was the discovery, in 1973, by Fischer Black, Myron S. Scholes and Robert C. Merton, of a way of actually calculating the option premium. Scholes and Merton were awarded the Nobel Prize in Economic Sciences in 1997 (Fisher Black died before the prize was awarded).

Finally, just like forwards and futures, options are traded on organized derivatives exchanges as well as over-the-counter. Unlike the situation in the forward market, however, all options share the same name (options).

8.3 Basic Option Terminology

In order to understand how options work, we need to introduce some basic option terminology. In fact, there is an arsenal of terms that we have to be familiar with before we can learn how options actually work.

First, there is the *underlying asset*, i.e. the asset that you have the option to buy or sell. A complete list of all possible underlying assets will not be presented here, simply due to the fact that more or less all reasonably well-standardized "assets" can be thought of as potential candidates. Instead, we will just list a selection of the most important assets that currently serve as underlying assets to options:

– *Stocks.* The major stock markets around the world are among the most liquid financial markets there are, and options on stocks give the investor an alternative way of gaining exposure to the stock market. Positive as well as negative exposure to the health of the stock market can be achieved through the stock options market,

© The Author and Studentlitteratur

Finance – Markets, Instruments & Investments

and the positions can be taken for both speculative and hedging purposes.

- *Stock Indexes.* A stock index is a portfolio of stocks, such as S&P500, which is an index that contains 500 large publicly held stocks that trade on the New York Stock Exchange (NYSE) and on Nasdaq. If you are looking for a quick and easy way of gaining exposure to entire markets, then stock indexes and options on stock indexes are natural tools. Due to the large number of stocks in the typical index (the underlying asset), index options are settled in cash.

- *Currencies.* This is one of the most common underlying assets in options contracts. At least in countries with floating currencies such as the US, the Euro-countries, the UK and Japan. Non-financial companies that manage cash flows in foreign currencies are important actors in the currency options market.

- *Interest rates (Bonds).* This is another important options market. The global debt market is huge, and the fluctuating interest rates observed in large parts of the world economy create a demand for tools to manage the resulting interest rate risk. The close link between bonds and interest rates makes bonds one of the most important underlying assets in options contracts.

- *Commodities.* More and more commodities are being used as underlying assets in options contracts. Examples range from classical commodities such as corn, sugar, gold and oil to more exotic ones such as wood pulp and pork bellies (tripe lovers might be less surprised than the rest of us). The basic requirement for a commodity to be suitable as an underlying asset is that it can be standardized. That is, paintings and other pieces of art cannot easily be used.

- *Electricity.* One of the latter markets to be commoditized is the market for electrical energy. In some of the more financially advanced countries electricity is traded on exchanges (such as NordPool in Scandinavia). This has created a demand for derivatives written on the electricity price. Although forward (futures) contracts dominate, electricity options are also available.

Finance – Markets, Instruments & Investments

Imagine an aluminum smelter, which is one of the most energy guzzling industrial processes there are; in a world where electricity prices sometimes rise five-fold in one single day, the owner of the smelter needs to manage the substantial price risk. Electricity options can be useful in such situations.

– *Weather.* This is one of the more novel options markets, but it is also a market with huge potential. The "wrong" weather can be detrimental for a company, or a country. Ski resorts depend on sufficient snowfall to make a living. Ice cream producers depend on the summer being warm enough to generate enough demand for ice cream. In poor countries, droughts (or floods) cause famines that, at least in theory, could be avoided if governments could insure themselves against too small (or large) amounts of rain by using options contracts. In short, options related to the amount of rain or snowfall in a certain area, the temperature in a certain city, or the hurricane activity in a certain region is one way of reducing weather risk. In all these cases the weather is the underlying "asset".

We stop short here, but as the reader understands there is almost no end to what can constitute an underlying asset in an options contract. Let us instead continue by defining some of the contractual details that appear in every options contract:

– *The exercise (strike) price:* the price that the buyer and the seller of the option have agreed on for the future exchange of the underlying asset. This price is often, but not always, chosen to lie quite close to today's spot price of the underlying asset. That is, a stock option where the underlying stock costs $10 today may have an exercise price equal to perhaps $9, $10 or $11.
– *The maturity date*: the future date when the actual exchange of the underlying asset is to take place. In organized options exchanges the maturity date could for instance be the third Friday in one of the following months. After this date the option cannot be used and it becomes worthless (it expires).

© The Author and Studentlitteratur

103

Finance – Markets, Instruments & Investments

- *The maturity:* the time left to the maturity date.

There are many different types/classes/states of options and a division of options into different categories is necessary. Here, we limit ourselves to two fundamental types, *call options* and *put options* (see below). In addition, both call and put options can be of American style or of European style:

- *American Options:* options that can be exercised at any date up to the maturity date. Notice that there is nothing "American" about American style options! In fact, there are American style options traded all over the world, including Europe and the US.[40]
- *European options:* options that only can be exercised at the maturity date. Again, there is nothing "European" about European style options!

It is important to understand the difference between these two contract styles. American options offer the owner everything that European options do *plus* the possibility of exercising the option early. Therefore, given the choice of one of two identical options with the only difference being that one is American and the other European, you should of course choose the American option.

We will now introduce the two core types of options, the call option and the put option:

- *Call options*: options that give the owner the right to *buy* the underlying asset. Many types of options are available in today's advanced financial markets, but this is the classic options contract. It is also the most important building block in more complicated (exotic) options contracts and most academic studies on options have focused on call options.
- *Put options*: options that give the owner the right to *sell* the underlying asset. Call and put options are identical except for the

---

[40] It is just an unfortunate choice of name.

104   *© The Author and Studentlitteratur*

Finance – Markets, Instruments & Investments

important difference that one gives you the right to buy something and the other gives you the right to sell something.

Finally, whether we are talking about call or put options or whether the options are of the American or the European type, there are always two counterparties involved in an options deal; one buyer and one seller:

– *The buyer (owner) of the option*: he/she has the *right* to purchase (if a call option) or sell (if a put option) the underlying asset for a certain price at a certain date(s) in the future. The buyer pays the seller for this right (option). The price is called the option premium and may be determined in various ways. The best known method is the Black-Scholes formula from 1973 (see section 8.7).
– *The seller of the option*: he/she *is obliged to* deliver (if a call option) or purchase (if a put option) the underlying asset to/from the option owner if the option owner decides to exercise the option. The future purchasing/selling price of the underlying asset is equal to the exercise price.

At this point, it should be obvious to the reader that there is a range of different combinations of all these different types and classes of options. The most important cases are:

– *You own (you are long) a call option* – you have the *right* to *buy* something…..
– *You have sold (you are short) a call option* – you have the *obligation* to *sell* something…..
– *You own (you are long) a put option* – you have the *right* to *sell* something…..
– *You have sold (you are short) a put option* – you have the *obligation* to *buy* something…..

As we will see in some detail in section 8.4, the riskiness of the four option strategies above is quite different. For example, the buyer of an option could never lose more than the option premium (that is already

© The Author and Studentlitteratur

105

Finance – Markets, Instruments & Investments

paid). The seller, however, can lose significantly more if he/she is unlucky. It all depends on the price movements of the underlying asset.

If we return to the option classification scheme, each of the four strategies above could be for American or European options, for options with long or short maturities, for options with high or low exercise prices and for options written on all kinds of underlying assets. Needless to say, it is easy to be confused when options contracts are discussed. However, if you just sit down and dissect the contract at hand in a systematic way, it is not really difficult, but just a question of being careful with the details.

We are not quite finished with our classification of different option categories! There is one more widely used classification that we need; any option can be classified according to how its (contractually fixed) exercise price is related to today's spot price of the underlying asset. This is called the option's degree of *moneyness*, and there are three "classes":

- *In-the-money* – immediate exercise of the option is worthwhile (the spot price is above the exercise price for a call option and below the exercise price for a put option).
- *Out-of-the-money* – immediate exercise of the option is *not* worthwhile (the spot price is below the exercise price for a call option and above the exercise price for a put option).
- *At-the-money* – the situation in between *in-the-money* and *out-of-the-money*. Immediate exercise of the option is *not* worthwhile (the spot price is exactly equal to the exercise price).

An option can move between being out-of-the-money and in-the-money over time if the spot price of the underlying asset trends up and down. In other words, an option that is currently out-of-the-money (and consequently not worthwhile exercising today) could very well become in-the-money with the passage of time. Hopefully, for the options buyer, this will happen before the option expires.

106   © *The Author and Studentlitteratur*

Finance – Markets, Instruments & Investments

8.4 Payoff Diagrams

In this section we will look at the *four* options strategies listed above, i.e. buying or selling call or put options. For each of the four strategies we will investigate the payoffs (and profits) to the options buyer/seller as a function of the underlying asset price. As an example we will look at a stock option on the firm Bioyama Corp.'s stock with an exercise price equal to $100. All the graphs below picture the payoff (profit) at maturity, i.e. on the exercise date. To link these payoffs to the option premium paid up front by the option buyer we will need the theory discussed in section 8.7. For the moment, however, let's focus on the payoff at maturity. As opposed to the option premium, the payoff is perfectly straightforward to derive.

We start with *call options*. Figure 8.1 below shows the payoffs to the call option buyer and seller at maturity, T, as a function of the underlying Bioyama Corp. stock price at maturity, S_T. As mentioned above, the exercise price, X, is $100 (fixed in the contract) and the option premiums of the call option, C, and the put option, P, respectively, are both assumed to be $10.

In Figure 8.1, the payoff (the cash flow) to the *buyer* of the call option is shown using a dotted grey line. In mathematical terms, the payoff at maturity can be written as

$$(S_T - X) = (S_T - 100) \quad \text{if} \quad S_T > X$$
$$0 \qquad\qquad\qquad\quad \text{if} \quad S_T \leq X$$

If the underlying Bioyama Corp. stock price at maturity is higher than the exercise price (the option is in-the-money), then the payoff to the Bioyama Corp. call option owner is the difference between the two. If, on the other hand, the stock price is lower than the exercise price (the option is out-of-the-money), then the payoff is simply equal to zero. The reason is that no rational owner of the call option would ever use the option if it is out-of-the-money. It is simply cheaper to buy the Bioyama Corp. stock directly in the spot market than through the option agree-

© The Author and Studentlitteratur

ment. The payoff has the shape of an ice-hockey stick and this non-linear property of the payoff is a very important property of options.

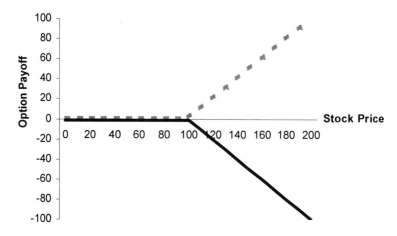

Figure 8.1 The payoffs, at maturity, to the buyer (dotted grey) and seller (black) of a call option.

The payoff at maturity is not the only cash flow relevant to the owner of the option. At some date in the past, he/she paid the seller a premium (compare an insurance premium) for the option to buy the stock at maturity (if the call option is of the European style) or at any date up to maturity (if the call option is of the American style). In order to find out whether the option buyer has made a profit or not, we first have to subtract the call option premium, C, from the payoff.[41] The net profit is shown in Figure 8.2 (the dotted grey line). In mathematical terms, the profit at maturity is equal to

$$(S_T - X) - C = (S_T - 100) - 10 \quad \text{if } S_T > X$$
$$0 - C = -10 \quad \text{if } S_T \leq X$$

If the option expires out-of-the-money, then the profit is actually negative. Only if the stock price exceeds the exercise price by more than

---

[41] We ignore the time value of money.

$10, i.e. $S_T > 110$, is the call option buyer making a profit. As can be seen in Figure 8.2, there is no limit to the potential profit of the call option buyer despite the quite small initial investment ($10). If the stock price goes up, so does the call option buyer's profit.

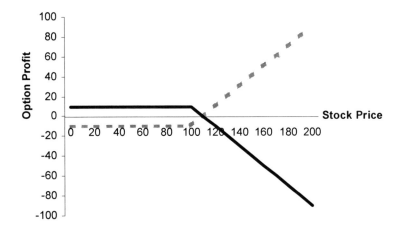

Figure 8.2 The profits, at maturity, to the buyer (dotted grey) and seller (black) of a call option.

If we continue to the *seller* of the call option, the payoff to the *seller* is shown in Figure 8.1 using a black line. In mathematical terms, the payoff to the call option seller at maturity can be written as

$$-(S_T - X) = (100 - S_T) \quad \text{if} \quad S_T > X$$
$$0 \quad \text{if} \quad S_T \leq X$$

If the call option's exercise price at maturity is lower than the price of the underlying Bioyama Corp. stock price (the option is in-the-money), then the payoff (which is negative) to the Bioyama Corp. call option seller is the difference between the two. If, on the other hand, the exercise price is higher than the stock price (the option is out-of-the-money), then the payoff is simply equal to zero. The reason is of course,

Finance – Markets, Instruments & Investments

again, that the call option in this case would never be exercised by the owner.

As for the buyer of the option, the payoff at maturity is not the only cash flow relevant to the seller of the option. At some date in the past he/she received the option premium from the buyer. In order to find out whether the option seller has made a profit or not we have to add the option premium, C, to the payoff. The net profit is shown in Figure 8.2 (the black line). Mathematically, the profit at maturity is equal to

$$(X - S_T) + C = (100 - S_T) + 10 \quad \text{if} \quad S_T > X$$
$$0 + C = 10 \quad \text{if} \quad S_T \leq X$$

If the option expires out-of-the-money, then the profit is positive. However, it is capped at $10. That is, for the seller of the option, the maximum profit is the option premium. On the other hand, if the stock price exceeds the exercise price by more than $10, i.e. $S_T > 110$, then the call option seller is making a loss. As can be seen in Figure 8.2, there is no limit to the potential loss of the call option seller, so selling call options is obviously a very risky business, at least if we measure the risk as the maximum possible loss (which is infinite). If the stock price goes up, the call option seller's loss increases.

Before we repeat the entire exercise above for put options, it is worthwhile observing that the total profit to the buyer and the seller is a zero sum game. Whatever the buyer wins the seller loses. This situation is reminiscent of Gordon Gekko (our old favourite from chapter 1) and another of his quotes in the film *Wall Street*:

> <u>*Bud Fox*</u>: *When does it all end, huh? How many yachts can you water ski behind? How much is enough?*
>
> <u>*Gordon Gekko*</u>: *It's not a question of enough, pal. It's a zero sum game, somebody wins, somebody loses. Money itself isn't*

Finance – Markets, Instruments & Investments

> *lost or made, it's simply transferred from one perception to another.*

Regardless of the validity of this point in general, or in the actual context in the film, it is at least like this for the buyer and seller of an options contract.

We will now continue with *put options*. Figure 8.3 below shows the payoffs to the put option buyer/seller at maturity, T, as a function of the underlying Bioyama Corp. stock price at maturity, S_T.

In Figure 8.3, the payoff (the cash flow) to the *buyer* of the put option is illustrated using a dotted grey line. In mathematical terms, the payoff at maturity can be written as

$$\begin{array}{ll} 0 & \text{if } S_T \geq X \\ (X - S_T) = (100 - S_T) & \text{if } S_T < X \end{array}$$

If the underlying Bioyama Corp. stock price at maturity is higher than the exercise price (the option is out-of-the-money), then the payoff to the Bioyama Corp. put option owner is zero. If, on the other hand, the stock price is lower than the exercise price (the option is in-the-money), then the payoff is simply the difference between the exercise price and the stock price.

© The Author and Studentlitteratur

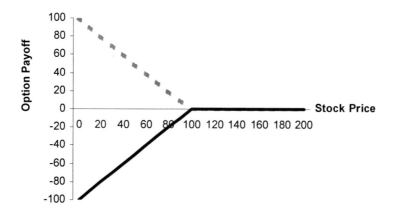

Figure 8.3 The payoffs, at maturity, to the buyer (dotted grey) and seller (black) of a put option.

Again, in order to find out whether the option buyer has made a profit or not we have to subtract the put option premium, P, from the payoff. The net profit is shown in Figure 8.4 (the dotted grey line). In mathematical terms, the profit at maturity is equal to

$$0 - P = -10 \qquad \text{if } S_T \geq X$$
$$(X - S_T) - P = (100 - S_T) - 10 \qquad \text{if } S_T < X$$

If the option expires out-of-the-money, the profit to the option buyer is of course negative. Only when the stock price is more than $10 cheaper than the exercise price, i.e. $S_T < 90$, is the put option buyer making a profit. As can be seen in Figure 8.4, the profit to the put option owner increases with a falling stock price. This is an interesting property of put options, and it is a property that is exploited by both speculators and risk managers.

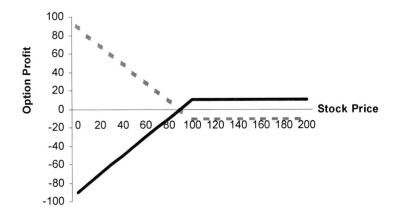

Figure 8.4 The profits, at maturity, to the buyer (dotted grey) and seller (black) of a put option.

If we continue to the *seller* of the put option, the payoff to the *seller* is shown in Figure 8.3 using a black line. In mathematical terms, the payoff to the put option seller at maturity can be written as

$$0 \quad \text{if } S_T \geq X$$
$$(S_T - X) = (S_T - 100) \quad \text{if } S_T < X$$

If the put option's exercise price at maturity is lower than the price of the underlying Bioyama Corp. stock price (the option is out-of-the-money), then the payoff to the Bioyama Corp. put option seller is zero. If, on the other hand, the exercise price is higher than the stock price (the option is in-the-money), then the payoff is equal to the difference between the stock price and the exercise price.

Again, in order to find out whether the option seller has made a profit or not we have to add the put option premium, P, to the payoff. The net profit is shown in Figure 8.4 (the black line). In mathematical terms, the profit at maturity is equal to

$$0 + P = 10 \qquad\qquad \text{if} \quad S_T \geq X$$
$$(S_T - X) + P = (S_T - 100) + 10 \qquad \text{if} \quad S_T < X$$

As can be seen in Figure 8.4, there is a limit to the potential loss of the put option seller $(P - X)$, so selling put options is obviously less risky than selling call options.

The archetype of a speculative position in the options market is to buy a call option. The possible profit is infinite and the potential loss is capped to the option premium. The archetype of a hedging position, on the other hand, is to combine a long position in a put option with a long position in the underlying asset. In this way one removes all risk and the cost of this risk reduction is equal to the option premium, P.

8.5 Put-Call Parity

This section discusses a relationship, called the *put-call parity*, which has to hold between call option and put option prices in an arbitrage-free market. The relationship is useful for pricing purposes as well as for setting up options strategies. We use the payoff diagrams in section 8.4, together with the arbitrage principle, to prove the parity. In the derivation below we assume that the underlying asset is an ordinary stock.

First, put-call parity only holds for European type options. Second, the options in the parity have to be written on the same underlying asset, have the same exercise price and the same maturity. If S is the underlying asset price (the stock price), C is the n-year maturity call option premium (price), P is the n-year maturity put option premium and X and r_f are the nominal amount and interest rate of a risk-free n-year maturity zero-coupon government bond, respectively, then the following relationship must hold

$$S + P = \frac{X}{(1 + r_f)^n} + C \qquad\qquad (8.1)$$

Finance – Markets, Instruments & Investments

If this relationship did not hold, there would be arbitrage possibilities available in the market. Put differently, the law of one price forces the left-hand side and the right-hand side of equation (8.1) to be equal; i.e. a portfolio of a stock and a put option is identical to a portfolio of a zero-coupon bond and a call option. This result is not obvious and we are now going to prove that this is actually the case using the payoff diagrams in the previous chapter.

If we can prove that the two portfolios, i.e. the left-hand side and the right-hand side in equation (8.1), give exactly the same payoff at maturity, then, since European options can only be exercised at maturity, the two portfolios must cost the same today. Otherwise the law of one price would be violated. The payoff to the left-hand side portfolio is illustrated in Figure 8.5.

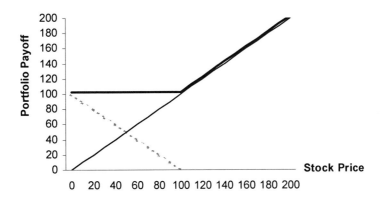

Figure 8.5 The payoff, at maturity, to the left-hand side portfolio; i.e. a put option plus a stock.

The put option payoff (the dotted grey line) is identical to that in Figure 8.3 and the payoff to the underlying stock (the thin black line) is of course represented by a 45° straight line from the origin (since the x-axis and y-axis in this case both represent the stock price). The total value to the portfolio is found by adding the two assets' payoffs. The total payoff is represented by the thick black line.

Finance – Markets, Instruments & Investments

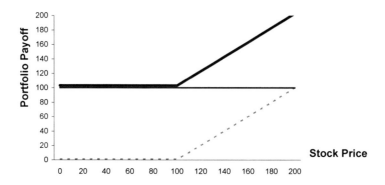

Figure 8.6 The payoff, at maturity, to the right-hand side portfolio; i.e. a call option plus a zero-coupon bond.

The payoff to the right-hand side, in turn, is pictured in Figure 8.6 and, again, the call option payoff (the dotted grey line) is recognized from Figure 8.1. The payoff to the zero-coupon bond (the thin black line), in turn, is simply a constant payoff equal to X regardless of the underlying stock price. This is quite obvious since zero-coupon government bonds have nothing to do with stocks and the payoff to any zero-coupon bond at maturity, per definition, is equal to the nominal amount. The total value of the portfolio is again represented by the thick black line. If we compare the total portfolio values in Figures 8.5 and 8.6, we see that the two are identical. In other words, the value, at maturity, of the left-hand side portfolio is identical to that of the right-hand side portfolio. Since European type options may only be exercised at maturity, this proves the put-call parity!

The put-call parity is a convenient tool that may be used, for instance, to price a put option on a certain asset if you have the price of a call option on the same asset.[42] In addition, the put-call parity can also be used to

---

[42] Again, both options have to be of European type and have the same maturity and exercise price.

Finance – Markets, Instruments & Investments

create *synthetic* options. That is, if there are no put options traded on, say, the Bioyama Corp. stock, only call options, then we can create a synthetic put option using the call option together with the stock itself:

$$P = \frac{X}{\left(1+r_f\right)^n} + C - S \qquad (8.2)$$

In words, by combining a long position in a call option, a short position in a stock and a long position in a government bond (or money in a bank account) you can create a synthetic asset (portfolio) with exactly the same properties as a put option.

We end this chapter with a tale of how the put-call parity allegedly was discovered.

Example 8.1
An interesting use of the put-call parity is to create synthetic assets; another is in circumventing government regulation. Legend has it that a certain 19th century businessman called Russell Sage was the first to use the relationship for these purposes. Government regulations at the time prohibited Mr. Sage from charging a high enough interest rate on a loan to a borrowing client. The clever Mr. Sage realized that if he bought a stock in any publicly traded company from the client, at the same time as he bought a put option and sold a call option on the very same stock, he could create a high-interest rate loan in disguise. The client took the opposite position in all the assets (he was the counterparty) and this, essentially, made him a borrower. The interest rate could be tailored to satisfy both Sage and the client and in this way Sage could charge the client an illegally high interest rate. Sage was happy, the client was happy and the government did not even know it was fooled! This is a nice lesson for two reasons. First, government regulation can often be bypassed by knowledgeable market participants. Second, a deep under-standing of the basic rules of finance can be very profitable.

© The Author and Studentlitteratur

8.6 What Determines the Option Price?

Up to this point we have assumed that the option premium (price) somehow is given to us as known. We have also avoided the question of which factors affect the price. That is, is the option price affected by changing interest rates, the underlying asset price, the exercise price, the maturity etc.?

Before we take on the task of pinning down the critical parameters needed to price (value) an ordinary option, it is important to understand the difference between the option's *total* value and its *intrinsic* value. The difference between the two is called the option's *time value*.

The *intrinsic value* is simply equal to the payoff you would receive if you exercised the option immediately:[43]

Call option: *The intrinsic value* = max[$S - X$, 0]
Put option: *The intrinsic value* = max[$X - S$, 0]

The more in-the-money the option, the higher its intrinsic value. Out-of-the-money options have zero intrinsic value. However, an option with time left to maturity always has *time value*, regardless of whether it is out-of-the-money or in-the-money. The reason is that any option with remaining time to expiration always has a positive probability of becoming in-the-money in the future (or more in-the-money), which is the reason for the positive time value. Now, the observant reader would argue that it is possible for the opposite to happen as well, i.e. an option that currently is in-the-money could become out-of-the-money. In other words, considering this possibility, why would the time value be positive? Now, the simple reason is the asymmetric shape of the payoff function. If an option is slightly in-the-money, like call option A, which has an exercise price equal to $100 and an underlying asset currently costing $105, then whether a price drop in the underlying asset is small

---

[43] Think about the option in this chapter as an American type option. The result is the same for European type options but the reasoning is somewhat different.

118 © *The Author and Studentlitteratur*

Finance – Markets, Instruments & Investments

or large does not really matter. As long as the price drop is larger than $5 the option becomes out-of-the-money regardless of whether the price drop is $6 or $60. A price increase, on the other hand, has a different effect on the option value. The more the underlying price increases the more the value of the option increases. Here, whether the price increase is $6 or $60 has a significant effect on the option value! It is this asymmetry that creates the time value. The slightly in-the-money call option A is marked with a dot in Figure 8.7 and as you can see its value is higher than the intrinsic value (the ice-hockey stick). Similarly, if the underlying asset's value fell to $95, then the value of option A would also fall. However, its value would not fall to zero since it still has its time value; there is always a chance that the option will become in-the-money, and whether it remains slightly out-of-the-money or becomes deep out-of-the-money does not really matter. The value of the option can never fall below zero! In this case, the slightly out-of-the-money option A is marked with a square in Figure 8.7. If we continued with this exercise for all possible underlying asset prices, we would end up with the curved option price function in Figure 8.7. This is the option price as a function of the underlying asset price and at this stage we only know that this curve lies above the payoff function (as depicted in Figure 8.7). The vertical distance between the two is the time value and right now we do not have the tools to calculate this value (see section 8.7 for more discussion on this). The reason for the option price starting at the origin is that the option value goes to zero if the underlying asset price goes to zero (the right, or option, to buy something with zero value for $100 is obviously not worth anything to the option owner). Likewise, the reason why the option price moves closer and closer to the payoff function as the underlying asset price increases is that the asymmetry loses importance to the option owner as we get further and further away from the kink in the (ice-hockey shaped) payoff function. Consequently, the time value to the option owner also diminishes.

© The Author and Studentlitteratur

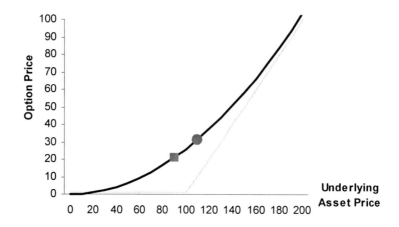

Figure 8.7 The option price (the black curve) as a function of the underlying asset price.

The underlying asset's price obviously affects the option price (see Figure 8.7). This is not the only factor that affects the option price, however, and a complete list of the factors is found in Table 8.1, where we see how the different factors affect the call option price and the put option price, respectively.

Factor (increase)	Call option price, C	Put option price, P
Underlying Asset Price, S	C↑	P↓
Exercise Price, X	C↓	P↑
Time to Maturity, T	C↑	P↑
Asset Price Volatility, σ	C↑	P↑
Risk-free Interest Rate, r_f	C↑	P↓

Table 8.1 A complete list of factors that affect the option price (option premium).

Table 8.1 contains a complete list of the factors affecting the option price (premium), but the reason why it is these factors, and not a different set of factors, is beyond the scope of this book. As we will see in section 8.7, these are the factors that appear in the Black-Scholes option pricing formula. For us, that will have to be enough of an argument.

Finance – Markets, Instruments & Investments

We may, nonetheless, try to convince ourselves that the effect of the factors on the options prices is as indicated in Table 8.1. First, the effect on the call option price of an increase in the underlying asset price is clearly positive (see Figure 8.7 or the payoff function) and, consequently, the effect on the put option is the opposite. Likewise, the effect of the exercise price on the option price is equally trivial (again, see Figure 8.7 or the payoff function). Furthermore, the reason for both the call option price and the put option price increasing with an increasing time to maturity is that the longer the maturity the more optionality the option owner has (again, think about American type options). The effect of the risk-free interest rate is a bit too complicated to discuss here but the link is luckily too weak to be of any real interest. The volatility of the underlying asset price (return), however, is very important. Not only is the volatility the only parameter in Table 8.1 that has to be estimated (calculated), but its effect on the option price is also surprisingly important. Both the call option and the put option prices have a positive dependency on the volatility; put simply, the more spread out the possible future asset value, the more valuable the option on that underlying asset. The reason is the earlier mentioned asymmetry of the payoff function, and an example might clarify this important point.

Example 8.1

Assume that you own a three-month-maturity call option on a certain kind of jet fuel called MC77.[44] Today's jet fuel price is $100 (per gallon) and in our simplified world there are only three possible (equally likely) future jet fuel prices, $90, $100 or $110 (per gallon) in three months' time. If your option has an exercise price equal to $100, then your option payoff in three months' time will be $10, $0 or $0 depending on whether the jet fuel price goes up, stays the same or goes down. In other words, *the average option payoff is approximately $3.33. The average future jet fuel price, meanwhile, is $100*. Now, assume that only one thing in this setup changes; the possible future prices of the jet fuel change to $50, $100 and $150 (per gallon). In other words, the jet fuel price has become much more volatile. *The average future jet fuel price is unchanged, however, at $100*. The payoff to the

---

[44] That is, you have an option to buy a certain amount of MC77 in three months' time.

© *The Author and Studentlitteratur*

Finance – Markets, Instruments & Investments

option owner is now $50, $0 or $0, i.e. *the average option payoff is now approximately $16.67.* What is the lesson here? Well, with an increasing volatility of the underlying asset, ceteris paribus, the average call option payoff increases, from $3.33 to $16.67. Therefore, the call option price must also increase with an increasing volatility. The same holds for put options and you can convince yourself that it is so by repeating the exercise above for a put option (or use the put-call parity).

8.7 Option Pricing – The Black-Scholes Formula

The put-call parity gives us the price of a call option if the price of the corresponding put option is known, and vice versa. However, this is not really that helpful since there is a circular logic behind it; if we cannot find the put option value, how on earth can we then find the call option value? Instead, what we need is a way of pricing call options and put options *independently* of each other. This is where the Black-Scholes formula enters the stage.

Until the early 1970s there was no consensus on how options should be priced. Many different suggestions on how to find the price of call and put options existed but none were correct. The situation changed completely with the publication of a research article in 1973 by Fisher Black and Myron S. Scholes, two young US economists. Their novel approach to the pricing of options was based on the good old arbitrage reasoning that we have encountered numerous times in this book. Black and Scholes found that it was possible to create a riskless portfolio containing an option and the underlying asset and that arbitrage would force the return from this portfolio to be equal to the risk-free interest rate. Based on this insight, the two developed the now widely used Black-Scholes formula.[45]

---

[45] It should be mentioned that another brilliant economist, Robert C. Merton, also made invaluable contributions to the development of this formula and to its extensions. Robert C. Merton was consequently awarded the Nobel Prize together with Myron S. Scholes.

122   *© The Author and Studentlitteratur*

Finance – Markets, Instruments & Investments

The Black-Scholes formula (or model) is not the only way we have to price options today but it is certainly the most elegant. The price is not 100% correct, since some of the assumptions are slightly unrealistic. The pricing error is very small, though, and the flexibility of the model far outweighs its shortcomings. Many alternative models have been suggested but, despite their added complexity, they show very limited improvements compared to the original model. This is the real proof of the ingenuity behind the formula and it has probably led to the Black-Scholes formula becoming one of the most widely used in the world.

The derivation of the Black-Scholes formula is far beyond the scope of this book but we think it is worthwhile at least stating the formula (for European *call* options):

$$C = N(d_1) \cdot S - X \cdot N(d_2) \cdot e^{-r_f (T-t)} \tag{8.3}$$

where

$$d_1 = \frac{\ln\left(\frac{S}{X}\right) + \left(r_f + \frac{\sigma^2}{2}\right)(T-t)}{\sigma\sqrt{T-t}}$$

$$d_2 = d_1 - \sigma\sqrt{T-t}$$

and where
C = the call option price (today, at t)
S = the underlying asset price (today, at t)
X = the exercise price of the option (fixed in the contract)
T = the maturity date of the option (fixed in the contract)
σ = the standard deviation (volatility) of the asset returns (has to be estimated)
r_f = the risk-free interest rate (today, at t)
$N(d_i)$ = the cumulative normal probability density function (i.e. the probability that a normally distributed random variable will be less than or equal to d_i).

© The Author and Studentlitteratur

Finance – Markets, Instruments & Investments

The formula is very compact and if it was not for the normal distribution values, you could calculate the price on the back of an envelope. With a computer, however, the calculation of the option price only takes a few milliseconds.

Finally, if you like puzzles, try to come up with a good reason why the expected future price development of the underlying asset (whether the option investor expects the underlying asset to go up or down in value) does not show up in the formula. This means that this piece of information, surprisingly, is irrelevant for the option price!

8.8 Summary

In the world of modern finance, the typical financial instrument representing the classical "insurance" contract is the *option*. Like forwards and futures, options are derivatives securities, but they give you the right, not the obligation, to buy or sell something in the future at some predetermined price. Options can be written on any kind of asset and are traded both over-the-counter and on exchanges. Furthermore, due to their optionality property, they are very useful for risk management as well as for speculation. With a certain initial capital investment, a position in the options market is much riskier (and potentially much more rewarding) than a position directly in the underlying asset. In this chapter we have only treated the two most basic options contracts, the call and the put (option). Still, the prices of these contracts are not as straightforward to find as, for example, the price of a forward contract. In fact, it was not until the Black-Scholes model was presented in 1973 that one could price simple call and put options at all. With this model anyone can now price an ordinary European-type call or put option using an advanced pocket calculator or a simple computer. The derivation of the Black-Scholes model is beyond the scope of this book but it is important to observe that this model, just like the forward pricing formula, is based on the law of one price.

9. Investment Portfolio Choice I: The Mean-Variance Framework

In the previous four chapters we discussed bonds, stocks, forwards and options, i.e. various financial instruments. In this chapter (and the next) we take a closer look at how *investment portfolios* of such instruments can be formed. An investment portfolio is simply a set of assets collected by an investor in order to produce as good a risk-return performance as possible. Basically, what it is all about is getting as high an expected return on your investments as possible, conditional on the associated risk not being too large. Or put differently; maximize your expected return given the risk, or minimize your risk given the return. The very important lesson that *you cannot maximize your expected return and minimize your risk at the same time* is called the *risk-return tradeoff*. This chapter is about trying to bypass this matter of fact as much as the market allows us. In order to do that we rely on the principle of *diversification,* and on some 55 year-old academic results by the Nobel laureate Harry Markowitz.

9.1 Investment Portfolio Choice – The Basics

The main issue in investment analysis is to find assets that we believe will give us as high a return as possible. However, since we are risk-averse by nature we would like to do it with a minimal risk exposure. There is nothing surprising about this. Unfortunately, however, the whole investment exercise is made complicated (and has become an academic discipline) by the fact that the expected return and the risk of a

© The Author and Studentlitteratur

125

Finance – Markets, Instruments & Investments

financial asset typically go hand in hand. So, in order to boost your return performance, you have to increase your risk exposure as well. This does not sound like an overly interesting issue to spend time contemplating; simply make up your mind on your level of risk tolerance and invest accordingly. The more risk-averse you are the less of a return you can expect.

Luckily, at least for us finance academics, there is a non-trivial twist to this problem. The twist is called diversification and the surprising result is that you can actually achieve superior returns through a clever mix of assets in your portfolio without increasing your risk exposure. In fact, in some cases diversification might even enable you to reduce your risk at the same time as your expected portfolio return is increased! Furthermore, the way of finding this clever mix is not hidden in the clouds; through a simple application of basic mathematical statistics one can show exactly what this investment portfolio should look like. As a result, all investors who share the same beliefs regarding individual assets' risks and expected returns will also choose the same portfolio of risky assets. Only the share of their total invested capital that they allocate to this, the risky part of their portfolio, will differ. Some investors will put a significant share of their wealth in a bank account and some will not put anything in this risk-free (and low-return generating) alternative. This is where the level of risk aversion enters the stage.

Your level of (financial) risk aversion is not something you have inherited from your parents. That is, it is not purely genetic and may very well change over your life cycle. If you have children, then you might be more hesitant to take on huge financial risks. If you know that you only have a couple years left to live, then you will probably be more inclined to put your money into a safe savings account rather than invest it all in stocks or real estate. Furthermore, as we have discussed before, your profession might also affect your level of financial risk aversion. If your job income is highly uncertain (or perhaps even correlated with the performance of the stock market), then you are likely to be more risk-averse when it comes to your investments. All these observations tell us

126   *© The Author and Studentlitteratur*

Finance – Markets, Instruments & Investments

that the definition of an optimal investment portfolio changes over time as well as across different investors. Nonetheless, as we will see below, all these portfolios, despite all their differences, have *one* thing in common. And that is that the risky part of the portfolio is the same (under certain assumptions) regardless of who the investor is. This is an extremely important result and the research leading up to it gained the Nobel Prize (shared with two others) in Economic Sciences for Harry Markowitz in 1990.

9.2 Portfolio Returns, Risks and Correlations

Chapter 4 dealt briefly with how one can reduce one's risk exposure through diversification. If an investor spreads his or her investments across many different assets, then he/she also reduces the risk of making large losses (remember the egg baskets). We saw that this was at the cost of a smaller chance of making large profits; if you put all your money into the best (ex post) performing stock you will of course maximize your profit. In other words, it was not a clear win-win situation. We will now look at a slightly different problem and this time actually encounter something of a win-win situation; you will be able to reduce the risk *and* improve your return.

We looked at investments in *individual* stocks in section 4.3 (see the example where we invested either in Ski-Sinistra stocks or in Ski-Destra stocks). Then, the *mean*, μ, and *standard deviation*, σ, of the individual stock returns were calculated using the following two formulas

$$\mu = E[R] = \sum_{i=1}^{n} p_i r_i \qquad (9.1)$$

and

$$\sigma^2 = E\left[(R - \mu)^2\right] = \sum_{i=1}^{n} p_i (r_i - \mu)^2 \qquad (9.2)$$

where p_i is the probability of the stock return being r_i.

© *The Author and Studentlitteratur*   127

Finance – Markets, Instruments & Investments

Now, instead of investing in individual assets, we set out to invest in several assets at the same time, i.e. portfolios of assets. And our goal is to calculate risks and rewards, i.e. *means* and *standard deviations,* of these portfolios' returns. Before we present the formulas used for this we need to introduce an important concept from the world of mathematical statistics, namely the concept of correlation. The correlation measure is used to quantify the degree of co-variation between two stochastic (random-like) variables. An example of such a co-variation between two random variables is that between two stocks on the London Stock Exchange or that between the temperature in London and Oxford. Nonetheless, it is not our intention to thoroughly discuss the concept of correlation in this book. To better understand the rest of this chapter, however, we will try to develop an intuitive feeling for what correlation is. The actual computation of the correlation coefficient, ρ, is described in the Appendix.

Imagine two stocks whose prices follow the patterns in Figure 9.1. These two stocks are obviously very closely related to each other; perhaps they are in the same industry, or perhaps they are based in the same geographical region.[46] In statistical language, these two stocks are *highly (positively) correlated* with each other. In fact, they are even *perfectly (positively) correlated.* Per definition, the correlation, ρ, can never be larger than $+1$ and it can never be lower than -1 (see the Appendix).

---

[46] Of course, this a stylized example. You will never find two stocks that move in such a correlated fashion. The same holds for the regularity of the stock price patterns. You will never find a real-life stock whose price follows such a nice wave-like pattern.

128   *© The Author and Studentlitteratur*

Finance – Markets, Instruments & Investments

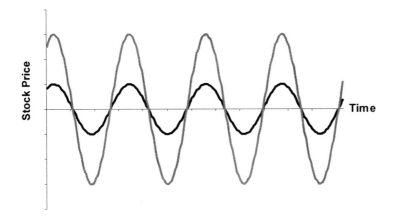

Figure 9.1 Price patterns of two perfectly correlated stocks.

In Figure 9.1, the two perfectly correlated stock prices have a correlation equal to *+1*, which is the maximum correlation that can be found between two stocks. Now, assume that two other stocks follow the patterns in Figure 9.2. This time the two stocks are obviously very weakly related to each other. In fact, they react in a completely reversed fashion. If the price of one of the stocks falls, the price of the other stock goes up, and vice versa. These two firms could be in two competing sectors, where the increased sales in one sector are completely counterbalanced by a reduction in sales in the other sector. In statistical language, these two stocks are *highly negatively correlated* with each other. In fact, they are even *perfectly negatively correlated*. In Figure 9.2, the two perfectly negatively correlated stock prices are said to have a correlation equal to *–1*.

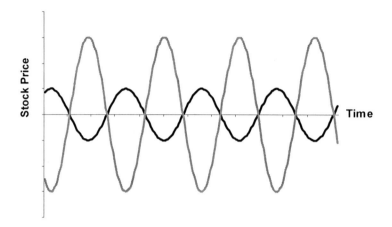

Figure 9.2 Price patterns of two perfectly negatively correlated stocks.

In addition to the two extreme cases, *+1* and *−1*, the correlation coefficient can take on any value in between. For example, the two stocks in Figure 9.3 move along completely *independently* of each other. These two stocks have a correlation equal to zero. They are said to be *uncorrelated*.

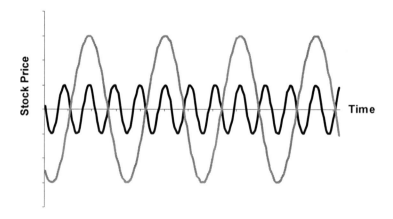

Figure 9.3 Price patterns of two uncorrelated stocks.

Finance – Markets, Instruments & Investments

Keeping the above, somewhat stylized, discussion on correlation in mind, we now present the equivalent to equations (9.1) and (9.2) but for portfolios instead of individual assets. For more background on why the formulas look the way they do, we refer you to any book on basic mathematical statistics. Furthermore, in what follows, we limit ourselves to portfolios with two assets a and b, and w_a and w_b are the portfolio weights of these two assets, respectively. That is, if $w_a = 0.4$ and $w_b = 0.6$, that simply means that *40%* of the portfolio investment is allocated to asset a and *60%* to asset b.[47] Then, the *mean, μ_p,* and *standard deviation, σ_p,* of the portfolio returns are calculated with the following two formulas

$$\mu_p = w_a \mu_a + w_b \mu_b \tag{9.3}$$

and

$$\sigma_p = \sqrt{w_a^2 \sigma_a^2 + w_b^2 \sigma_b^2 + 2 w_a w_b \sigma_a \sigma_b \rho_{a,b}} \tag{9.4}$$

where μ_a and μ_b are the means and σ_a and σ_b are the standard deviations of the two assets a and b, and where $\rho_{a,b}$ is the correlation between the two assets. As we will see below, the size of $\rho_{a,b}$ is of crucial importance for the actual portfolio choice and for the amount of diversification that can be attained by investing in more than one asset.

9.3 The Mean-Variance Framework

In this section we discuss the portfolio choice problem in some detail. As we have seen in earlier chapters, there are numerous kinds of financial assets available to include in a portfolio. All through the section, however, we limit ourselves to the bank account (or a risk-free government bond) and stocks (real estate, options, art, stamps, old Audemars Piguet pocket watches, etc. are not considered). This limitation is not necessary,

---

[47] Of course, the two weights always sum to one, i.e. $w_a + w_b = 1$.

© *The Author and Studentlitteratur*

Finance – Markets, Instruments & Investments

but it simplifies the problem. Still, if you like, you can replace the "stock" in the portfolio problem below with a more general "risky asset".

The modeling framework that we describe here is sometimes called the mean-variance framework, and the reason is that we focus on the means and variances of the asset returns in the asset portfolio.[48]

The basic idea of the mean-variance framework is to maximize the expected return (the mean) of the investment portfolio given a certain risk level (the standard deviation, or variance) of the investment portfolio. Essentially, to move as far up to the *northwest* in the μ_p-σ_p diagram (see below) as possible. In the derivation of an optimal portfolio that follows, we divide the portfolio choice problem into two steps:

1. *Find the optimal combination of stocks (risky assets).*
2. *Combine this optimal portfolio with a suitable amount of money in the bank account (the risk-free asset).*

9.3.1 The optimal combination of two stocks

We start with step one, i.e. finding an optimal combination of stocks. Initially, we limit ourselves to two assets. The more general case, with any number of risky assets, will be described *qualitatively* in section 9.3.4.

If we combine two stocks in a portfolio, the expected portfolio return and its standard deviation will naturally depend on the proportions in which you split your investment.[49] Do you invest a small share of your total investment in stock *a* and a large share in stock *b*, or vice versa? Or perhaps you invest 50% in each asset? Regardless of the proportions, however, the portfolio's expected return, μ_p, and volatility, σ_p, will be

---

[48] Remember, the variance, σ^2, is the square of the standard deviation, σ.

[49] This holds regardless of the correlation between the two stocks. At this point, however, we assume that the correlation between stock *a* and stock *b* is less than perfect, i.e. $\rho < 1$.

132   © *The Author and Studentlitteratur*

given by equations (9.3) and (9.4), respectively. If we vary w_a from 0 to 1 (and, accordingly, w_b from 1 to 0), we can draw the curve in Figure 9.4. Here, we leave the analytical derivation of this curve to the interested reader; simply solve for μ_p as a function of σ_p in the system of equations (9.3) and (9.4).

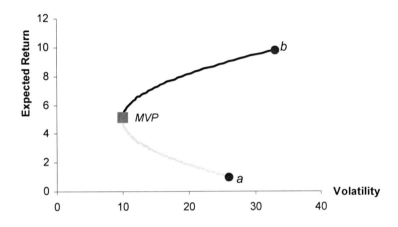

Figure 9.4 The portfolio frontier. The efficient frontier is represented by the solid black curve.

This curve is called the *portfolio frontier* (the risk-return trade-off curve) and the reason it is curved, and not a straight line, is the non-linearity of equation (9.4). All feasible portfolios containing the two stocks a and b will be found somewhere along this curve. Regardless of how you combine the two assets there is no way that you can end up anywhere else. At least as long as you do not take a negative (short) position in any of the two stocks. The two individual stocks, a and b, are marked with black dots.

Our aim is to choose the optimal combination out of all these (infinitely many) combinations of w_a and w_b. At this point, this is not trivial, and the only thing we can say is that it has to be somewhere along the upper (black) part of the curve. This segment of the portfolio frontier is called

Finance – Markets, Instruments & Investments

the *efficient frontier*. Each portfolio along this segment of the curve is efficient in the sense that it dominates the portfolio with the same risk at the lower (dotted grey) segment of the portfolio frontier at the same time as it itself is not dominated by any other portfolio. Therefore, no rational investor would ever buy the portfolios along the dotted grey curve; they would always prefer the ones on the efficient frontier.

This far, we have only been able to narrow down the feasible portfolio choices. However, we still have an infinite number of portfolios to choose from on the efficient frontier (infinity divided by two or three or any other number is still infinity...). The missing link is the risk aversion of the investor. To pin down the combination chosen by a particular investor we need to know the investor's risk aversion. Clearly, the more risk-averse the investor, the further to the *west* in the diagram he/she will position him/herself. For instance, the really risk-averse investor might choose the *minimum variance portfolio*, *MVP*, i.e. the portfolio with the lowest possible risk (measured by its standard deviation). The *MVP* is marked with a square in Figure 9.4. Unfortunately, at this point there is not much more to be said and the risk aversion discussion is better left to a later stage. In order to proceed, however, we need to introduce the risk-free asset, and that will be done below (the second step).

Before we proceed to the second step in the portfolio choice process, a very important observation needs to be stressed further. If you compare the *MVP* portfolio with portfolio *a* (the low-risk stock), you immediately see something very interesting. By giving up some of the relatively low-risky *a* stock in favor of the more risky *b* stock, you actually *reduce* your portfolio risk! The minimum variance portfolio (*MVP*), for instance, has *both* a higher expected return and a lower risk than the *a* stock. This is the win-win situation we have talked about before and it is a conse-quence of the diversification attained when combining many stocks. It looks like magic but it is a pure outcome of the less than perfect correlation between the two stocks (see section 9.3.5). This is the free-lunch-like feature of diversification that we talked about in earlier chapters.

Finance – Markets, Instruments & Investments

9.3.2 The optimal combination of the bank account and *one* stock

We now temporarily leave the situation where we have many risky assets (stocks) and instead focus on the case where we only have one stock and one risk-free asset (the bank account). In this case the mathematics is simple enough for us to explicitly solve for the μ_p-σ_p trade-off (compare section 9.3.1 where we left it to the interested reader). Here, equation (9.3) becomes

$$\mu_p = w_1\mu_1 + w_2 r_f = w_1\mu_1 + \left(1 - w_1\right)r_f \tag{9.5}$$

and equation (9.4) becomes

$$\sigma_p = \sqrt{w_1^2\sigma_1^2 + (1-w_1)^2\sigma_2^2 + 2w_1(1-w_1)\sigma_1\sigma_2\rho_{1,2}} \tag{9.6}$$

where r_f is the risk-free interest rate, μ_1 is the expected return of the stock, and $\rho_{1,2}$ is the correlation between the two assets. Since one of the assets is the bank account, which has a *known* return (i.e. it is not a stochastic variable), we can simplify (9.5) and (9.6). First, since the return to the bank account is known, its volatility, σ_2, is equal to zero. And second, since the return is a constant variable, and not a stochastic variable, the correlation $\rho_{1,2}$ is also equal to zero. Equation (9.6) therefore becomes

$$\sigma_p = w_1\sigma_1 \tag{9.6'}$$

and by solving for w_1 in (9.6') and inserting it into (9.5) we end up with the following nice and simple expression for the μ_p-σ_p trade-off

$$\mu_p = r_f + \left(\mu_1 - r_f\right)\frac{\sigma_p}{\sigma_1} \tag{9.5'}$$

© *The Author and Studentlitteratur*

This equation, known as the *capital market line* (CML), describes the possible risk and returns attainable by investing your money in a combination of the savings account and one stock.[50] The CML is illustrated in Figure 9.5 (for $r_f = 2\%$) and just like in section 9.3.1 we cannot proceed any further at this point. The optimal choice among all the portfolios along the CML depends entirely on the investor's risk aversion and the more risk-averse he/she is the more he/she will invest in the bank account (i.e. the more he/she will move to the *southwest*).

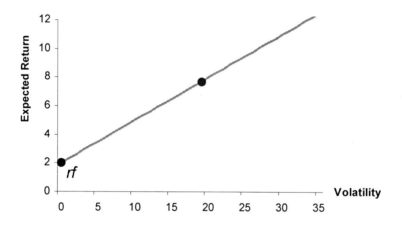

Figure 9.5 The capital market line (CML).

9.3.3 The optimal combination of the bank account and *two* stocks

We still have not found what we are looking for, i.e. the optimal portfolio. In order to proceed we have to diversify among stocks *and* include the risk-free asset. In other words, we have to combine the findings in section 9.3.1 with those in section 9.3.2. This will be represented with a straight line (the *capital market line* in section 9.3.2) *and* a curve (the *portfolio frontier* in section 9.3.1). The question is just

---

[50] Some of you might recognize the CML as the equation for the straight line in your high-school mathematics course.

Finance – Markets, Instruments & Investments

how the two geometric shapes should be drawn together in one diagram. Basically, since our task is to combine all three assets (the two stocks and the risk-free bank account), it all boils down to choosing the point along the portfolio frontier to which the straight line should connect. Figure 9.6 demonstrates one possible solution where the bank account is combined with a portfolio of the two stocks *a* and *b* in proportions given by point *K*.

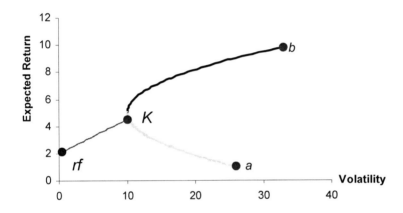

Figure 9.6 The "capital market line" and the portfolio frontier.

The observant reader might ask him/herself why we have connected the straight line (called the "capital market line" if you like) to this particular point, i.e. *K*. Would it not be better to connect the straight line to a point further up the curve, such as *L* in Figure 9.7?

Finance – Markets, Instruments & Investments

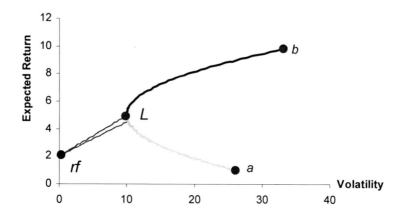

Figure 9.7 The "capital market line" and the portfolio frontier.

The answer is yes, and the reason is of course that all (three-asset) portfolios along the $r_f\text{-}L$ line dominate the (three-asset) portfolios along the $r_f\text{-}K$ line (since the expected returns for the $r_f\text{-}L$ portfolios are higher than those for the $r_f\text{-}K$ portfolios, despite identical risk). If we repeat the whole thing over and over again, we will eventually end up with an optimal line, the *tangent*, that cannot be improved upon. See Figure 9.8. This line, $r_f\text{-}M$, that connects the risk-free asset (the bank account) with the *tangency portfolio*, M, is what will be called the *capital market line* (CML) from now on. The CML connects the risk-free asset with the *optimal portfolio*, M, of risky assets (stocks), so the portfolios along this line are therefore also optimal. All of them! What we have found is not one optimal (three-asset) portfolio but a whole range of optimal (three-asset) portfolios. They are all as far up to the *northwest* as possible and which one the investor ultimately prefers will depend on his or her risk aversion. We will come back to this, the ultimate portfolio choice, in section 9.4.

Finance – Markets, Instruments & Investments

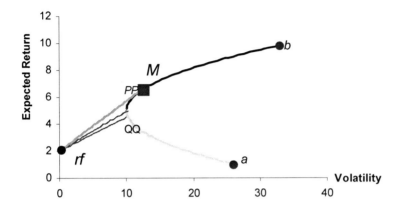

Figure 9.8 The optimal portfolios (two stocks that are combined in a portfolio with the risk-free asset) all lie along the capital market line (CML).

Note that all the feasible portfolios elsewhere in the μ_p-σ_p space are dominated by the CML portfolios. For instance, the investor (not one of us) who buys the portfolio called *QQ* is clearly worse off than the investor (one of us) who chooses the CML portfolio to the *north* of *QQ*, i.e. *PP*. The two portfolios have the same risk, but *PP* has a much higher expected return than *QQ*.

Criticism is sometimes directed against choosing investment portfolios according to the mean-variance framework. This critique is based on the argument that you will never be rich fast enough if you choose this strategy. If your only goal is to get rich as fast as possible (and you are therefore prepared to take huge risks), buying a portfolio containing thousands of stocks will not suffice. Instead, the argument goes, you need to put all your eggs in the same basket, and hope for the best! Now, this critique is not relevant, and the reason is that nothing stops you from borrowing lots of money and investing it all in *M*. In this case, what you are actually doing is taking a negative position, $w_2 < 0$, in the bank account (you borrow money instead of deposit money) and a very large position, $w_1 > 1$, in *M*. This is of course a very risky strategy, but if you manage to borrow enough money you can make huge profits if the *M* portfolio performs well enough.

9.3.4 The optimal combination of the bank account and *many* stocks

The optimal portfolios in section 9.3.3 were, admittedly, somewhat unrealistic since they only contained two risky assets (stocks). In real life, professional investors usually create portfolios containing hundreds, or perhaps even thousands, of stocks. Luckily, the portfolio choice problem does not change, in principle, if we include more stocks in our optimization algorithm above. We simply repeat the analysis in section 9.3.3, but with the two stocks *a* and *b* replaced by hundreds or thousands of stocks. The analysis becomes more complex, of course, but the end-result is the same. Each of the many thousands of combinations of two stocks (or two portfolios of stocks) will create a new curve in the diagram and the result will look something like Figure 9.9. Instead of one single curve we will have a surface made up of thousands of curves. The interesting result is that the surface will be delimited by a curve (the border) that looks exactly like the curve in Figure 9.8. Therefore, all the results in section 9.3.3 also hold for the more realistic multi-stock case.

Finance – Markets, Instruments & Investments

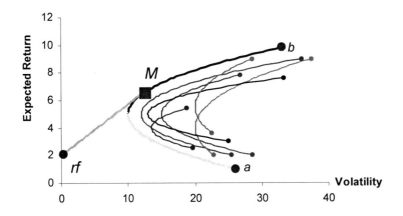

Figure 9.9 The optimal portfolios (many stocks that are combined in a portfolio with the risk-free asset) all lie along the capital market line (CML).

9.3.5 The effect of various levels of correlation

The correlation between the risky assets was crucial for the results above, and the portfolio frontier in Figures 9.4 through 9.9 was drawn with a correlation between the two stocks that was less than $+1$. That is, the two stocks were *not* perfectly correlated. If they were, there would be no diversification gains to collect since both stocks would always move in the same direction in reaction to news. It is like an international investor who has to choose two stocks and chooses *Coca-Cola Co.* and *PepsiCo*. In fact, despite being highly correlated, not even these two stocks are perfectly correlated.

If we constructed the portfolio frontier with a different correlation between the two stocks it would look something like Figure 9.10. Here, there are at least two very important lessons to be learned. First, if the correlation is $+1$, i.e. perfect correlation, then the portfolio frontier degenerates into a straight line. In this case there are no diversification profits to be made, and the curve/line combining the two stocks does not bulge towards the *west* (as we would like it to). Second, the lower the correlation (the further away from $+1$ we move) the more the portfolio frontier bulges to the *west*. Hence, as an investor we would prefer to diversify between two stocks that are as weakly correlated as possible. The ideal situation is to invest in two assets that move in separate directions in reaction to news. An example could be Norwegian oil company stocks and US automobile company stocks. Again, even these stocks are far from perfectly negatively correlated.

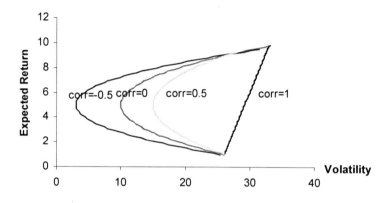

Figure 9.10 The portfolio frontier for different levels of correlation between the two stocks.

9.4 Two-Fund Separation

In section 9.3 we found a whole range of optimal portfolios. All the portfolios along the CML were optimal in the sense that they were not dominated by any other portfolio. One thing that was common to all these portfolios, however, was the risky portion. As mentioned before, all the CML portfolios in Figure 9.9 contain the same portfolio of stocks! The only thing that differs among the various CML portfolios is the amount of the total investment in stocks and the amount that is left in the risk-free bank account (or the government bond). If all the money were invested in the tangency portfolio, M, then, and only then, would you ultimately end up at point M in Figure 9.9. This is where the least risk-averse investor would end up (as long as he/she is not allowed to borrow

Finance – Markets, Instruments & Investments

money). If you were extremely risk-averse, on the other hand, you would put all your money in the bank account and end up at point r_f in Figure 9.9. All the investors with risk-aversions between these two extremes would end up along the CML; the more risk-averse, the more to the *southwest*.

This can be summarized as follows:

> *All investors, regardless of their degree of risk aversion, who agree on the expected returns and risks of individual risky assets choose the same portfolio of risky assets, M, to combine with the risk-free asset.*

In other words, the degree of risk aversion enters the picture only when the investor eventually has to decide how much risk he or she is prepared to live with. Regardless, he/she will always invest in a combination of *M* and the bank account, nothing else.[51] This finding is important enough to merit its own name and it is sometimes called *two-fund separation.*[52]

As a result, the portfolio choice has now been reduced to two separate steps:[53]

1. *The risky part of the portfolio has to be constructed along the lines above.*
2. *A decision has to be made on how much of the total investment is to be allocated to the risky part.*

The nice thing about this is that the difficult part of the portfolio choice problem (step 1, the creation of *M*) can be outsourced to experts, such as

---

[51] It is important to remember, however, that the concept of risk aversion is fundamental. If investors were risk neutral, then the results would be completely different.

[52] Notice that the term two-fund separation is sometimes used for other phenomena as well.

[53] Of course, these are not the same *steps* as those in section 9.3.

© The Author and Studentlitteratur

Finance – Markets, Instruments & Investments

investment banks, fund managers and the like, and you and me and all other investors only have to decide on how much risk to expose ourselves to (step 2, deciding the proportions of M in our final portfolio). The fund manager does not have to care about individual investors' risk aversion and the investors do not have to care about all the many thousands of individual stocks' expected returns, standard deviations, correlations and the actual mathematical solution of the optimization problem. This is a very nice and important result, and in chapter 10 we will build on this to get even nicer, and possibly even more important, results!

9.5 Summary

Diversification is, in a sense, the only free lunch in the economy, and in this chapter we have discussed to what extent risk-averse individuals can profit from diversifying their investment portfolio. The main result is that the portfolio choice problem may be divided into two steps; the creation of an optimal portfolio of risky assets and the combination of this portfolio with the risk-free asset in proportions determined by the investor's degree of risk aversion. The first step can be "out-sourced" to firms specializing in constructing optimal risky portfolios and the second step can easily be implemented by the investor him/herself. Of course, this division of the portfolio choice into two separate steps makes the risky part of the investors' portfolios identical, at least as long as they agree on means, variances and correlations among the individual assets. This finding will be drawn upon in the next chapter where the capital asset pricing model (CAPM) will be discussed.

10. Investment Portfolio Choice II: The Capital Asset Pricing Model (CAPM)

The portfolio choice results in the previous chapter are truly important, and the insight given by the mean-variance analysis is of crucial significance to the general investor. Even if one does not adhere fully to the results in one's investment strategy, the general message on the merits of diversification is crucial. One problem with the mean-variance approach described above, however, is that you need to optimize your portfolio over thousands of risky assets. Not only is the actual optimization somewhat cumbersome, due to the size of the mathematical problem, but the estimation of all the many thousands of individual assets' means and variances is probably even more of a problem for the typical investor. One solution to the problem is to set up a more general model, with new assumptions, and see if you can simplify the actual portfolio choice problem somehow. The *capital asset pricing model* (CAPM) is such an attempt and will be discussed in this chapter. The CAPM is an equilibrium model and, like the mean-variance model, a Nobel Prize winning model.

10.1 CAPM – The Basics

We will not go through a detailed derivation of the capital asset pricing model (from now on called CAPM) in this book. Nor will we discuss, at any length, the assumptions that were made in the derivation. It is important to remember, however, that the CAPM is a model, and, like any model, it is based on various assumptions.

© The Author and Studentlitteratur

Finance – Markets, Instruments & Investments

The CAPM is an equilibrium model, equating demand and supply for various assets, the prices of which are determined by market equilibrium. This makes the CAPM different from the setup in the previous chapter, where we limited ourselves to *individual* investors trying to maximize their return while keeping the risk at a minimum. Instead, we now let all the investors interact in the market and then simply pick up the results that come out of this interaction. In equilibrium, the investors will invest in a way that makes the prices of all the assets adjust to their equilibrium levels. Furthermore, just like in the previous chapter, all investors will invest in the same risky portfolio. Now, though, we can immediately identify the common portfolio as the *market portfolio* (which will be defined below). This observation makes the actual implementation of the capital asset pricing model much easier than the implementation of the mean-variance model. No optimization is needed in order to find the optimal combination of risky assets, and the individual investors do not need to estimate hundreds or thousands of means and variances.

Before we continue to the model's major assumptions and implications we will look at how the CAPM tackles a question that in a sense summarizes the general idea behind the CAPM:

> *What would risky assets' risk premiums be in equilibrium if all investors had the same risk and return expectations and chose their investment portfolios optimally according to the principles of diversification?*

The answers are

1. *Since there is a price on risk and investors are risk-averse, the risk premium of **the aggregate of all the risky assets** must be positive.*
2. *Risk that can be diversified away (unique risk) is not priced and the risk of an individual asset therefore can not be priced in isolation. The risk premium of **an individual risky asset***

146   *© The Author and Studentlitteratur*

Finance – Markets, Instruments & Investments

> *must be determined by the asset's contribution to the risk of a well-diversified portfolio.*

The answers might appear somewhat cryptical at this stage. The main message, however, is that we have to separate *diversifiable risk* from *non-diversifiable risk*. Diversifiable risk is sometimes called *unique risk* or *firm-specific risk* and non-diversifiable risk is sometimes called *market risk* or *systematic risk*. The easiest way to think about the difference between the two types of risk is along the lines of chapter 9. There, we saw that the risk of a portfolio of two (less than perfectly correlated) stocks could be lower than the risk of either of the two individual stocks. That is, the risk of the portfolio was lower than the average of the two stocks' stand-alone risks. We called this nice result from the mixing of assets the *gain from diversification*. If we proceeded in this fashion and combined all the stocks in the world into a single portfolio, the risk of the portfolio would be significantly lower than the average risk of all the individual assets. The risk left in the (well-diversified) portfolio is called non-diversifiable risk, which is the risk that cannot be removed, regardless of how many stocks we include in the portfolio. Since the portfolio makes up the entire market, this risk is sometimes called market risk. The risk of the individual assets, however, consists of both the market risk *and* the stock's own unique risk. That is, an individual stock's total risk is made up of non-diversifiable risk plus diversifiable risk, and the message of the CAPM is that an investor is only compensated for the non-diversifiable part of the total risk! And the reason for this is that any rational investor is simply expected to diversify (since it is a free lunch).

The CAPM was independently derived by John Lintner, Jan Mossin, William Sharpe and Jack Treynor in the mid-1960s. In 1990, Sharpe was awarded the Nobel Prize in Economic Sciences for (among other things) this model. The actual derivation is quite long and technical and beyond the scope of this book. However, even if we have given up stringency in favor of readability, it is important to be aware of the major assumptions of the CAPM:

© The Author and Studentlitteratur

- *All assets are traded in markets.*
- *There are no transaction costs or taxes.*
- *All investors*
  - *– are price takers (small)*
  - *– are rational*
  - *– have homogenous expectations and share the same information*
  - *– are mean-variance optimizers*

Again, remember that CAPM is a model and, as such, its implications will never be more realistic than its assumptions. The most important assumption is that investors are supposed to behave according to the mean-variance model in the previous chapter, i.e. the investors are *risk-averse* and are prepared to take on more financial risk only if they are compensated by higher expected returns. They do not all have the same *degree* of risk aversion, though.

10.2 General Implications

One major implication of the capital asset pricing model (CAPM) is the composition of the individual investor's portfolio.

In equilibrium, all investors will hold the same relative quantities of the various risky assets as those in the market portfolio.

There are two points to stress here. First, the fact that all investors hold the same relative proportions of risky assets is not surprising, considering their homogenous expectations and information. Second, a portfolio called the market portfolio is central in the CAPM.

The market portfolio is simply the portfolio that contains *all* the risky assets in the world. Furthermore, each individual asset's weight in the portfolio depends on its total market value in relation to the total market value of all assets. Small companies enter the market portfolio with smaller amounts than large companies.

Finance – Markets, Instruments & Investments

Example 10.1
Suppose that our world was very small and harbored only four companies: IMB, Citron, Zoony and Fata. Furthermore, if the market value of IMB was $50 billion, the market value of Citron was $30 billion, the market value of Zoony was $15 billion, and that of Fata was $5 billion, the market portfolio would consist of 50% IMB, 30% Citron, 15% Zoony and 5% Fata. In other words, the smaller companies (measured by market value) would enter the market portfolio, but with smaller amounts than the larger companies.

Considering the implication above, the following must also hold:

CAPM assumes that all investors are mean-variance optimizers and therefore choose optimal portfolios. Furthermore, in equilibrium, all investors will hold the same relative quantities of the various risky assets as those in the market portfolio. Therefore, the market portfolio must be optimal and lie on the capital market line (CML).

The important implication of this is that, since all the investors are fully diversified according to the mean-variance model, *the tangency portfolio, M,* in the previous chapter must be identical to *the market portfolio!* Basically, we are back to the results in the mean-variance framework, but with the somewhat hard-to-find *M* portfolio replaced with the very-easy-to-find market portfolio.

Furthermore, the following equation must hold between the expected return on a portfolio i, μ_i, and the expected return on the market portfolio, μ_{market}

$$\mu_i = r_f + \left(\mu_{market} - r_f\right)\frac{\sigma_i}{\sigma_{market}} \qquad (10.1)$$

r_f is the risk-free interest rate and σ_i and σ_{market} are the standard deviations (volatilities) of the portfolio and the market portfolio, respectively. This is the *capital market line* (CML) as CAPM defines it. The CML is found in

© *The Author and Studentlitteratur*

Figure 10.1 (where the market portfolio is assumed to have an expected return, μ_{market}, equal to 8% and a volatility, $\sigma_{market,}$ equal to 20%). Notice that the mathematical formulation is the same as that in chapter 9 (equation 9.5'); the equation describes a straight line connecting the risk-free bank account and a risky asset (portfolio). And again, the investor has to choose a portfolio along this line, i.e. combine the risky portfolio with the risk-free asset. The only new thing is that the risky portfolio is now the easily defined market portfolio.

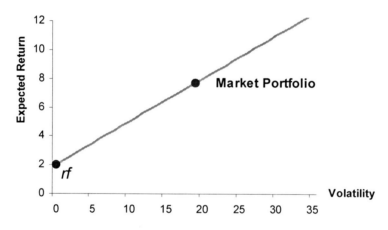

Figure 10.1 The capital market line (CML).

An important implication of the result above is that the market portfolio is optimal. This, in turn, implies that a *passive investment strategy* is as good as any other strategy. In fact, a passive investment strategy is even *optimal*. It is simply a strategy where one splits one's investment between the risk-free savings account and a portfolio containing as many of the existing risky assets as possible (in proportions to their total market value). The latter can be accomplished in a quick and easy way with an index

Finance – Markets, Instruments & Investments

fund.[54] In other words, there is no point trying to beat the market through stock picking.[55] Instead, you are better off dividing your money between the index fund and the bank account and in that way creating your own optimal portfolio somewhere along the CML.

Another important implication of the CAPM is that investors only need to carry market risk, without having to expose themselves to firm-specific risk. Furthermore, the more market risk the investor is exposed to, the higher the expected return he or she gets on his/her investment. The volatility of the investment, σ_i, in equation (10.1) is a measure of the risk, and this risk (and the expected return, μ_i) can only be increased by buying more of the market portfolio. Therefore, in order to get a better performing portfolio, the investor has to take on more market risk. The market realizes this and does not compensate investors for investing in less diversified portfolios that actually carry more risk (both the market risk and the firm-specific risk). Thus, one of the implications of the CAPM is that investors diversify as much as possible (to get rid of the non-compensated firm-specific risk), and that it is sub-optimal for the investor to concentrate his/her investment to a *small number* of risky assets.

---

[54] Many banks and fund managers provide such funds (portfolios) to the public. Their arguments for why you should buy these funds are, indirectly, the very results implied by the CAPM.

[55] Skilled investors might of course occasionally be able to (temporarily) beat the market, but competition between investors will force them back to the CML over time.

© The Author and Studentlitteratur

Finance – Markets, Instruments & Investments

10.3 Risk Premiums on Risky Assets

In addition to the result concerning market risk and passive investing above, one of the most important implications of the CAPM is the introduction of an alternative risk measure called β and its ability to determine the risk premium on an individual risky asset.

A risky asset's risk premium is simply the extra return the market requires on the asset, compared to the risk-free interest rate offered by the risk-free asset. For example, if the risk-free interest rate is 3% and the return required (expected) by the market to invest in a certain risky asset, like the stock of the travel agency Luna-Viaggi S.p.A., is 7%, then the risk premium on Luna-Viaggi S.p.A. is 4%.

According to the CAPM the following must hold for the risk premium on a risky asset:[56]

> *The risk premium on a **risky asset, i,** is a function of the covariance, $\sigma_{i,m}$, between the asset and the market portfolio:*
>
> $$\mu_i - r_f = \beta_i (\mu_{market} - r_f) \text{ where } \beta_i = \sigma_{i,m} / \sigma^2_{market}$$

In a way, the equation in the statement above has become synonymous with the CAPM; even though CAPM is an entire modeling framework, most people know of it as a mere equation, namely $\mu_i - r_f = \beta_i (\mu_{market} - r_f)$. The equation contains a new risk measure, β, which is one of the most intriguing facts about it. Just like the volatility, σ, the β-value is a risk measure associated with an individual risky asset (both σ and β are zero for the risk-free asset).[57] However, while the volatility, σ, of an asset may be estimated on its own, the β-value has to be estimated taking the rest of the market into consideration. We hope the reader recognizes this line of reasoning from section 10.2 where we stressed the role of the entire market in determining the risk of optimal port-

---

[56] Again, a full motivation for this statement is beyond the scope of this book.

[57] The market portfolio, per definition, has a β-value equal to one.

152   *© The Author and Studentlitteratur*

folios. Again, we are faced with a statement stressing the role of the market, even when we are actually interested in the risk premium of an individual asset.

It should be stressed that in the CAPM framework the β-value is the correct risk measure to use for individual assets, not the volatility! Furthermore, in equilibrium, the risk premium on any risky asset is known as soon as the asset's β-value is estimated; the higher the β-value the higher the risk premium. The equation describing this risk-return trade-off is called the *security market line* (SML)

$$\mu_i = r_f + \beta_i (\mu_{market} - r_f) \tag{10.2}$$

The security market line is shown in Figure 10.2 and should not be confused with the capital market line (CML). While both lines are implied by the CAPM, they carry different messages. While any asset, optimal portfolio or not, can be found on the SML, only efficient portfolios (i.e. those made up of the market portfolio and the bank account) can be found on the CML.

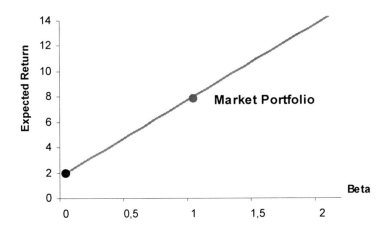

Figure 10.2 The security market line (SML).

Finance – Markets, Instruments & Investments

Finally, the reason for high-β assets having a higher risk premium than low-β assets is simply that high-β assets help the investor less with accomplishing diversification (since they have a higher correlation with the rest of the assets). If the investor includes a high-β asset in his or her already partly diversified portfolio, then that asset contributes less towards full diversification than a low-β asset (a high-β asset adds more risk to the portfolio than a low-β asset). Since theory (CAPM) says that investors should diversify, they will prefer low-β assets to high-β assets and they will therefore be prepared to pay more for the former. All things equal, the more expensive low-β assets would then give the investor a lower expected return (as implied by equation (10.2)).

10.4 Portfolio Choice

As mentioned above, an important implication of the CAPM is that the market portfolio is optimal. A passive investment strategy is therefore also optimal; split your investment between a risk-free savings account and a portfolio containing as many of the existing risky assets as possible (in proportions to their total market value). This may be summarized as follows:

According to the CAPM you should diversify the risky part of your portfolio so that it resembles the market portfolio.

As mentioned above, this particular portfolio choice could be achieved with one of the many *index funds (index-tracking funds)* provided by the typical fund manager. If, for some reason, you cannot find a global index fund, you can simply add up a number of regional index funds, each covering a certain region such as Russia, Latin America or Asia.

The passive investment strategy has been hard to beat in empirical tests. When active portfolios have been compared to passive portfolios with the same volatility, the passive ones have often out-performed the actively managed portfolios. This is an indication of the validity of CAPM.

Finance – Markets, Instruments & Investments

Moreover, the passive strategy is also cheaper than active strategies; if you look through the prospectus of a fund manager you will typically find that index-tracking funds are cheaper than actively managed funds. As a result, the passive investment strategy advocated by the CAPM is not only theoretically appealing, but it is cheap to implement and has a good track record.

10.5 Stock Pricing

A stock pricing model called the *dividend discount model* (DDM) was derived in chapter 6. According to the DDM, today's stock price should be equal to the present value of all the stocks' expected future dividends. To simplify the actual implementation of the model, we made an additional assumption and ended up with another model called the *constant growth rate* DDM. In this model the dividends are assumed to grow at a constant growth rate, *g*, over time and the stock price is given by

$$P_0 = \frac{D_1}{k-g} \tag{6.7}$$

where P_0 is the *price* of the stock today and D_1 is the *expected dividend* in one year's time. The discount factor, *k*, is called *the market discount rate* and in chapter 6 we referred to this chapter, and the CAPM, for a way of determining *k*.

Moreover, in chapter 3, when discussing discounting, we made a distinction between discounting risk-free and risky cash flows. The former should be discounted with the risk-free (bank–account) interest rate while the latter should be discounted with a *risk-adjusted discount rate* (reflecting something called market risk). We are now in a position where we know what the market risk is, and the only thing that remains is to determine how the risk-adjustment should be carried out in practice. The risk-adjusted discount rate is of course identical to the market

© The Author and Studentlitteratur

155

discount rate, k, and if we can determine k we can also price stocks using the DDM or the constant growth rate DDM.

According to the CAPM, the market expects a return on stock i that is equal to

$$\mu_i = r_f + \beta_i \left(\mu_{market} - r_f \right) \tag{10.2}$$

if the stock has a risk equal to β_i. Since the DDM was derived with k equal to the stock return expected by the market (see chapter 6), we may simply identify k with μ_i:

$$k = \mu_i = r_f + \beta_i \left(\mu_{market} - r_f \right) \tag{10.3}$$

We are now in a position to price a stock using the CAPM. Before we turn to an example of this elegant, and widely used, approach to pricing stocks, it is important to ponder a little upon the reasoning behind the method. A question one might ask oneself is the following: why does unique risk not enter the pricing model? Should the owner of a very volatile asset not be compensated with a very high return? Or stated differently, why does the volatility of the asset not appear in the pricing formula above? Well, first of all, remember that this pricing method is one of many results coming out of a model, the CAPM. And as you should know by now, one of the assumptions of the CAPM is that investors diversify. Therefore, if you, for some reason, decide *not* to diversify and instead purchase just *one* volatile asset, then you are actually not behaving very rationally if all other investors *do* diversify. Basically, you (who do not diversify) are left with a very risky investment that might still very well give you a very small return since the risk of the asset (for all other investors who do diversify) might actually be very low. That is, all other investors measure the risk using β, and the β-value of the asset might actually be very low, despite the volatility of the asset being quite high. Since the β-value is low, it

Finance – Markets, Instruments & Investments

follows that the risk premium in equilibrium is low (SML), that the price of the asset is high and that you are fooled….

Example 10.2

Let us return to Example 6.1 and the Russian firm Kalas-Nikov. In Example 6.1 we wanted to price a Kalas-Nikov stock using the constant growth rate DDM. The dividend growth rate was estimated to be 2%, next year's dividend was estimated to be 5 Ruble and the risk-free interest rate was 3%. How do we estimate (calculate) the market discount rate, k? By using the CAPM of course! What we need to estimate first, however, is the β-value of the Kalas-Nikov stock, which may be done in different ways using the history of stock prices and *econometrical* methods. This is beyond the scope of this book, however, and we simply assume that we have somehow managed to estimate β to be equal to *1.7*. Using the β-value of *1.7*, together with an estimate of the expected return on the market portfolio that is equal to 5%, we can calculate the market discount rate using the CAPM:

$$k = \mu_i = r_f + \beta_i\left(\mu_{market} - r_f\right) = 0.03 + 1.7(0.05 - 0.03) = 0.064$$

Today's Kalas-Nikov stock price, P_{today}, should therefore be

$$P_{today} = \frac{D_1}{k - g} = \frac{5}{0.064 - 0.02} \approx 114 \text{Ruble}$$

If the market is perfectly described by the CAPM and if the market on average, like you, estimates the β-value to be *1.7*, then 114 Ruble should be the actual price in the market place. Of course, in reality the price might differ more or less from this one.

10.6 Summary

One of the most important lessons to be learned from reading this chapter is that a passive investment strategy could very well be as good as an active (stock picking) strategy. At least that is one of the implications of the CAPM modeling framework. The CAPM also stresses the concept of the market portfolio, and the passive investment strategy suggested by it is implemented by combining this market-wide

© The Author and Studentlitteratur

Finance – Markets, Instruments & Investments

portfolio of risky assets with the only risk-free asset, the bank account. Furthermore, the CAPM introduces a new risk measure, β, in addition to the classical risk measure, σ. While the volatility, σ, is the appropriate risk measure for an optimal portfolio of the market portfolio and the risk-free asset, the β-value is the appropriate risk measure for all individual assets. The risk premiums on individual assets are given by the assets' β-values, and the more risk the asset contributes to a well-diversified portfolio the higher the return it will be expected to generate. Or stated differently, investors are rewarded by higher returns only by taking on more market risk (non-diversifiable risk). The asset's unique risk (firm-specific risk) is irrelevant. Finally, the risk-return trade-off of individual assets is given by the security market line (SML) while the risk-return trade-off of optimal portfolios is given by the capital market line (CML).

11. Market Efficiency

Are stock prices predictable? Are there any patterns to be found in time-series of historical gold price movements? And if so, can we use these regularities to make a trading profit? If the answer to any of these questions is yes, then that particular market is said to be *inefficient*. More exactly, in inefficient markets, market prices do not correctly represent the true values of the assets. Is there any support for typical financial markets being either efficient or inefficient? Unfortunately, there is no clear-cut answer to this question, and in this chapter we will try to shed some light on this efficiency-inefficiency controversy. This ambivalence makes this chapter fundamentally different from the other chapters in this book. Basically, it is the only chapter where finance experts do not agree on the issues at hand. In some respects this also makes the concept of market inefficiency particularly exciting.

11.1 Are Markets Efficient?

All through this book we have assumed that market prices, whether we are talking about highly liquid currency markets or exotic electricity derivatives markets, always fully reflect the true value of the asset at hand. Simply put, we have assumed that prices, at all times, are "correct". The same holds for finance as a discipline; almost without exception markets are always explicitly, or implicitly, assumed to be *efficient*. The reason for this is partly convenience and partly empirical evidence. If the asset price were not tied to the intrinsic value of the

© The Author and Studentlitteratur

159

Finance – Markets, Instruments & Investments

asset, it would be very difficult to develop financial theories.[58] And even if the finance community is not in agreement on whether markets are really efficient or not, there is ample evidence that they are.

To answer the question of whether markets are efficient or not we first need to define the very concept of efficiency. The definition that we will use in this book is the following:

A market is said to be efficient if the market price fully reflects all available information.

Of course, to test whether this statement holds or not we need to define what is meant by *all available information*. In doing so, it is common to define three different "levels" of information

- **historical information**: *all the historical price movements*

- **public information**: *quarterly reports, analysts' letters, credit-ratings, macroeconomic data etc.*

- **insider information**: *secret information that only insiders (such as company CEOs) have*

These three levels of information, in turn, are associated with three different levels of efficiency

- **weak efficiency**: *the price reflects all historical information*

- **semi-strong efficiency**: *the price reflects all public information*

- **strong efficiency**: *the price reflects all information, including insider information*

---

[58] It should be mentioned that a new strand of financial literature, called *behavioral finance*, has evolved over the last ten years or so. Behavioral finance does not make the same market efficiency assumptions as classical finance theory. We will not treat behavioral finance in this book.

160   *© The Author and Studentlitteratur*

Finance – Markets, Instruments & Investments

Note that the stronger the efficiency the more difficult it is to make money in the market, based on information-driven buy and sell decisions. In a strongly efficient market not even insiders can predict future price movements. And if a market is semi-strongly efficient, then you cannot make money by predicting the direction of the asset price even if you base your trading decision on all public information. Except by chance, that is. Furthermore, insider information obviously contains all public information in addition to any secret information, and all public information also contains the price history of the asset. Therefore, if a market is semi-strongly efficient it is also weakly efficient etc. Or stated differently, if all public information is incorporated into the price, then, per definition, the entire price history is also incorporated.

We will now try to answer the main question of this chapter; i.e. is the market efficient or not? A cautious answer that many finance professionals would agree with is the following:

*Markets are **probably** weakly efficient and **possibly** also semi-strongly efficient!*

It cannot be stressed enough, however, that opinion is divided. In general, academics (university professors) are more inclined to support this statement than practitioners (stockbrokers, analysts, fund managers and the like) who are generally more in favor of the thought that market prices *can* be predicted. In addition, some markets (such as the $/Yen currency market or the US Treasury bond market) are likely to be much more efficient that others (such as the Vietnamese stock market or the Norwegian salmon futures market). Furthermore, most markets are becoming more efficient with time. Nonetheless, we will not go into a detailed market-by-market discussion here. It is more the job of speculators to try and find the inefficient markets and make a killing in the process. If there were just one market whose inefficiencies the author knew enough about to be able to exploit it, be sure that he would not tell you which market it was....

© The Author and Studentlitteratur

11.2 Weak Market Efficiency

If a market is *weakly efficient*, you cannot predict future market prices using the price history. Essentially, in such a market tomorrow's price movement has nothing to do with today's price movement. In mathematical language this price behavior is sometimes called a *random walk*. We can summarize this discussion using the following triangle:

Weak efficiency   —   *Prices follow a random walk*

\   /

Prices cannot be predicted using the price history

That is, if a market is weakly efficient, prices move randomly and future price movements are independent of past price movements. The implication of this is that investors cannot make money (over and above the return as compensation for the risk exposure) by analyzing the historical pattern of prices. Except by chance, of course.

Some people are surprised to hear that the more efficient a market is the more random-like the price movements are. It sounds pretty unlikely that a market where prices jump around in a random-like fashion is a much better functioning market than one where prices move in a smooth and predictable way. This is a mistake that even individuals who should know better sometimes make. It is not uncommon to hear business journalists expressing regret about a certain stock price jumping around seemingly irrationally. There is nothing that says that prices are irrational just because they change significantly from day to day. Of course, it *is* possible that prices change for no real reason, but it is more likely that a typical stock, at least in the larger and more liquid stock markets, moves around due to new information reaching the investors. In fact, the better the market works the quicker new information is incorporated into the market prices. This proposition can be summarized as follows:

Question: *Why do prices in an efficient market move around, seemingly, at random?*

Finance – Markets, Instruments & Investments

> **Answer:** *In an efficient market, price changes are caused by new information being released + Information flows randomly* $\Rightarrow$ *Prices move randomly!*

In an efficient market, all available information is always immediately incorporated into the market price. If, furthermore, all information comes randomly, then prices also have to move randomly. Since news, arguably, comes randomly (news does not always come at the same hour each day, it does not alternate between being positive and negative, it does not cluster around certain days of the week etc.), this makes a randomly moving price a sign of health rather than a sign of problems.[59] That is, the price is moving randomly, but not irrationally. It should be stressed, however, that in this context random does not mean trend-less. Naturally, if you purchase a stock, you typically expect a positive return as compensation for your risk. This means that, *on average*, the price of a stock trends upwards. The more risky the stock, the faster the price can be expected to rise. Never forget, though, that this is only true on average. You can never say with *certainty* that the stock price will go up.

As an analyst you might not care much for the discussion above. The only thing you care about is picking the stocks that will perform very well and including them in your investment portfolio. However, if markets are weakly efficient, you as an analyst cannot rely entirely on price movements to carry out your stock picking. You have to make your decisions based on other pieces of information. Locking yourself into a dark room with a computer screen showing nothing but the price history of the stock will not be a good strategy. You will not only develop possible vitamin deficiencies and other nutritional or social disorders, but you will also continuously lose money on fees and other transaction costs. The activity of trying to detect patterns in historical price series is

---

[59] It is important to stress that *good* or *bad* news really means *better than expected* or *worse than expected* news, and nothing else. For example, if a company reports better results than it did last year, but the market expected the results to be *much* better than last year, then the news, according to the market, is actually bad news.

© *The Author and Studentlitteratur*

Finance – Markets, Instruments & Investments

called *technical analysis* and, bluntly put, weak market efficiency makes technical analysis a completely pointless activity. The same holds for all other time-series methods that could be applied to asset price modeling. Again, a complete waste of time!

The possible irrelevance of technical analysis hinges upon markets actually being weakly efficient. Are markets indeed weakly efficient, one might ask? If the statement in section 11.1 is correct, the answer is yes, of course! But how could then technical analysis be such an important area of finance? How come big bulge bracket banks, including some (maybe all) of the largest US investment banks, have their own armies of technical analysts? Does it not signal something completely different from *the efficient market hypothesis*? It certainly does! Unfortunately, this is where opinion differs. At the same time as the big banks spend time and money on technical analysis, a lot of academic research, produced by some of the most influential researchers all around the world, signals that markets in general are pretty efficient. No consistent patterns are found in price series, and the patterns that do seem to appear are more a consequence of the human mind mistakenly seeing patterns where there are no patterns, rather than true profit-indicating patterns.

We will not be able to solve this controversy here, so we will simply leave it at that. Personally, though, I find the idea that you can sit comfortably at home or in a Wi-Fi hotspot in Chiang Mai (you do not have to sit in a dark closet....) and invest in the markets, using nothing but historical price series, an extremely seductive one. Unfortunately, it might simply be like the good old saying, *if it is too good it probably is too good to be true!*

To summarize, there is no consensus on whether prices in the major financial markets are predictable or not using historical price movements. Basically, it is best to believe in what you see with your own eyes, and if you happen to walk around with your eyes shut, at least

Finance – Markets, Instruments & Investments

remember to ask the analysts (technical or fundamental) to put their wallets where their mouths are.

We end this section with an example from the real world.

Example 11.1
There are numerous ways of playing the stock market. One of the more appealing is to import scientific findings from other disciplines to the art of stock picking. A friend of mine, for example, is using so-called *Fibonacci* numbers to try and predict turnarounds in the Swedish stock index market (OMXS30).[60] The numbers are well known to anyone who has read the bestseller *The Da Vinci Code*. They have also been well known to mathematicians for fifteen hundred years or so. Fibonacci numbers are intimately related to the *golden ratio* and they appear surprisingly often in nature. For instance, many shells, flowers and even perfect human faces demonstrate the same properties, i.e. those of the golden ratio or the Fibonacci numbers (not very surprisingly, the proportions of Elizabeth Hurley's face are consistent with the golden ratio while John Cleese's are not...). Even Leonardo da Vinci used these proportions in his early sixteen century drawings for the book *De Divina Proportione*! The idea is that if the Fibonacci numbers appear so frequently in nature, why should they not appear in stock price plots as well? After all, stock prices are produced by humans and humans seem to have an innate affection for the proportions described by the Fibonacci numbers. The golden ratio, which is intimately related to the series of Fibonacci numbers, is around 1.62 and the whole idea is to buy the stock index (through an index-tracking fund) when the price falls by a factor 1.62 from the latest high. Or more exactly, buy the index a couple of days before to get in ahead of the rest of the (uninformed) crowd who, without really knowing why, will start buying the index a couple of days later. The reason for their sudden urge to buy the falling stock is that they think the price has fallen *enough* since it has passed the 1/1.62 threshold.

In theory there is nothing wrong with the idea. When the crowd starts buying, you as a Fibonacci investor will make a healthy profit. The question is just whether it will work in practice; for instance, the Fibonacci

---

[60] I would like to stress that this friend is *not*, and I repeat, *not* a certain Dr Byström!

© The Author and Studentlitteratur

165

Finance – Markets, Instruments & Investments

numbers are not exactly new. And my friend is not the first mathematician trying to escape a meager job market through the help of a good old friend called the stock market. This far, however, at least as far as I know, my friend has not made it big time!

11.3 Semi-Strong Market Efficiency

Semi-strong market efficiency simply means that you cannot predict future market prices even if you use all available public information. Stated differently, market prices reflect all available public information, such as yearly company reports, central bank interventions, business cycle developments, historical price movements, etc. As a result, whether you use technical analysis, fundamental analysis or a combination of the two, you still cannot beat the market. If you invest in the stock market, for example, it is not enough to consider a company "good" if everyone else agrees it is "good". In that case the price of the company is already "high". Instead, the best strategy is to invest passively, i.e. to invest in a combination of the risk-free investment and the market portfolio (according to the CAPM).

Due to the massive amount of available information, it is very difficult to test for semi-strong market efficiency. One way of testing for this level of efficiency is to narrow down the amount of information, perhaps by focusing on a certain piece of information such as the profit in firms' quarterly reports. If the stock prices of a large number of firms are collected around their reporting dates, one may investigate the average reaction of the stock price at the reporting date. If all the firms whose profits are better than expected are collected in one group, and the average stock price reaction is studied, then anything but a sudden positive jump in the stock price is a sign of some kind of inefficiency. The same may be applied to any kinds of events, news of which is likely to be spread to the market, e.g. interest rate hikes, dividend payments, stock splits or mergers of firms. Generally, the results of such studies indicate fairly efficient markets. The results of the academic studies are not as overwhelmingly positive as in the case of weak efficiency, though.

Finance – Markets, Instruments & Investments

11.4 Strong Market Efficiency

Strong market efficiency, finally, is more or less impossible to test since the amount of information is not only huge but partly secret as well. On the other hand, there is no real reason to test for strong efficiency since most agree on typical markets *not* being strongly efficient. In fact, if markets were strongly efficient we would not need insider laws since not even insiders could beat the market using their secret information. Not even the CEO of a firm or a central bank chairman could in that case use his or her special information (the contents of tomorrow's yearly report or the decision in this afternoon's interest rate committee) to make a profit. For all practical purposes, however, markets are not strongly efficient, i.e. insiders *can* make money on their information if they decide to do so.

On the other hand, insider trading is illegal in most countries and that makes the question of strong efficiency or not more of a philosophical one. What if insiders are prohibited from making profits by law (punishments being severe enough to prevent insiders from actually using their information advantage)? Does that mean that the market is efficient? Furthermore, it also depends on where you draw the line. What should constitute insider information? Is the analyst who reads between the lines in an interview with the CEO of a large corporation an insider?

11.5 Stock Market Anomalies

Up to now we have discussed market efficiency in the context of aggregated information. Furthermore, all discussions have been fairly general, in the sense that the results have been valid for any market type, whether we are talking about stock markets, currency markets or wheat futures markets. In this section, however, we will discuss some *stock market* specific anomalies.

© The Author and Studentlitteratur

Finance – Markets, Instruments & Investments

In stock markets all around the world, financial researchers have found certain interesting regularities that should not exist if markets were efficient. We will look briefly at four of these anomalies:

- *The small firm effect*
- *The January effect*
- *The day of the week effect*
- *The P/E effect*

Each of these effects, if it truly exists, would indicate a breach of market efficiency.

The first one, the *small firm effect,* simply says that stocks of small firms give higher returns than stocks of other firms. This is claimed by many studies to be an empirically observed fact, even after the risk of the stock, which might very well be higher for small firms, is acknowledged. One reason for this somewhat peculiar result could be that stocks of small firms are less liquid than those of large firms, and that investors therefore require a liquidity premium to buy the small stocks. Another reason could be higher transaction costs for small firm stocks.

The second effect, the *January effect,* says that stock returns, on average, are higher in January than in other months. One reason for this empirically observed pattern could be taxes. If loser stocks are sold in December just to reduce taxes (through set-off), then the prices of these stocks will go up when they are bought back in January. That, in turn, will pull up the entire stock market. Another reason for the January effect could be the small firm effect; small firms seem to be over-represented among the stocks sold in December for tax reasons.

The third effect, the *day of the week effect,* says that the days of the week demonstrate (statistically) significantly different historical average returns. This is an empirical fact even when the weekend is taken into account (Friday to Monday is 72 hours, not 24 hours). The reason for the

168   © *The Author and Studentlitteratur*

Finance – Markets, Instruments & Investments

day of the week effect is unknown. On the other hand the effect is usually small.

The fourth effect, the *P/E effect*, says that companies with low P/E ratios (price over earnings ratios) give a higher return to the stockholder than other companies. This effect seems to be closely related to both the small firm effect and the January effect; i.e. it is particularly significant among small firms in January.

The stock market anomalies listed above indicate a certain degree of inefficiency that could possibly be used to make a profit through stock picking. We will now list four reasons for why this, after all, might not be the case:

– Often, the anomalies are too small to be economically profitable. When transaction costs and analysis costs etc. are considered, the profits disappear. *In practice, therefore, the markets are efficient.*
– When the anomalies become common knowledge, as they are today, they have a tendency to disappear. The market participants exploit the anomalies and in doing so they force them to disappear. *In practice, therefore, the markets are efficient.*
– The excess return of the stocks could be compensation for some factor other than market risk. Bankruptcy risk could be one explanation. *In practice, therefore, the markets are efficient.*
– Finally, we have to ask ourselves if we can trust the published academic studies. Only studies that find significant results are published (in good journals) and that makes the playing field slightly biased. The lack of a theoretical explanation for the anomalies puts further doubt on the relevance of the studies. *In practice, therefore, the markets are efficient.*

Ergo, the well known stock market anomalies listed above might simply be illusions. If so, this is another strong indication of market efficiency. We would like to finish by quoting a well-known global investor:

© The Author and Studentlitteratur

Finance – Markets, Instruments & Investments

*I measure what is going on and I adapt to it. I try to get my ego
out of the way. The market is smarter than I am so I bend!*

11.6 Summary

In this chapter we have discussed whether prices in financial markets
fully reflect all available information. Different levels of efficiency have
been introduced; weak, semi-strong and strong efficiency. The answer is
not clear-cut but a lot of research points in the direction of major
financial markets being fairly efficient, at least semi-strongly efficient.
As a consequence, neither technical nor fundamental analysis pays off,
and active portfolio strategies (stock picking) are useless. You are better
off choosing stocks by throwing darts at the stock company listings in
the business newspaper, and the only profitable strategy is the passive
one. In fact, the more efficient the market, the stronger the argument for
passive investment. An interesting problem with this line of thinking,
however, is that in order to be efficient a market must attract some active
investors. Otherwise, market prices will never fully reflect the available
information. But, then, what attracts the active investors to the efficient
market in the first place? The more efficient a market the less interesting
it is to the active investor. In other words, if the market is efficient it will
only attract passive investors, and turn inefficient in the process.....and
so on.

12. Credit

In chapter 5 we treated the debt market and basic instruments traded in that market. Throughout the major part of that chapter, however, we assumed that the loans and bonds were risk-free. That is, we assumed that the debt was issued by a large country that, with certainty, would pay back the loan. In finance language, the borrower was supposed to lack credit risk. In practice, however, many countries as well as most companies actually do constitute credit risks. As a result, they have to convince the market that they will pay back the loan, or honor whatever obligation they have to their counterparties, and ultimately have to pay a higher interest rate than the credit risk-free country. Basically, the riskier the borrower is considered by the market, the higher the interest rate it will have to pay.

The market for credit-risky loans, bonds and other debt-related instruments has grown very fast over the last five to ten years and so has the need for managing the associated credit risk. Moreover, while banks are exposed to many different kinds of risks, credit risk is by far the largest one. This, on its own, has resulted in banks spending a lot of time and money on managing credit risk. New regulatory rules, the so-called Basel II rules, have also speeded up the development of new approaches to dealing with credit risk. Credit derivatives, in turn, are the market's response to the growth in overall credit risk exposure, and these new financial instruments, together with the Basel II rules, have put more focus on the major credit rating agencies, Moody's, Standard & Poor's and Fitch. All these developments have occurred in parallel and in this chapter we discuss the basic features of this quickly expanding area of finance. The growing importance of the field has turned the group of

© The Author and Studentlitteratur

171

different credit-risky financial instruments into an asset class in its own right, called *credit*.

12.1 Corporate Bonds

If a country, bank or any other company wants to borrow money it may choose between turning to a bank for an ordinary bank loan or issuing bonds in the capital market.[61] Obviously, in doing so the borrower will try to minimize his/her borrowing costs, i.e. the borrowing (interest) rate. *Most countries*, except perhaps the most credit-worthy ones such as the US, Luxembourg, Norway and Switzerland, have a non-zero probability of having to cancel their debt repayments (due to serious economical/ political problems). The same holds for virtually *every company*, large or small, and these non-payments by the borrower are often called *defaults*.

All loans and bonds issued by defaultable entities, whether countries or companies, therefore bear an interest rate above the risk-free rate (which for the sake of simplicity may be considered to be identical to the US borrowing rate). The difference between the risk-free interest rate and the credit-risky interest rate is called the *credit spread*, which is the most important object of study in *credit* (i.e., the area of finance dealing with credit-risky counterparties).

In this book we will call all bonds issued by credit-risky entities (companies as well as countries) *corporate bonds*.[62] The important difference between corporate bonds and risk-free government bonds is the additional credit spread charged by the corporate bond investor. The spread is supposed to be large enough to compensate the lender for the small possibility that the borrower will stop making coupon payments or

---

[61] Private individuals cannot normally issue bonds. One notable exception is David Bowie who in 1997 issued bonds backed by his future record sales. Later on, several other artists followed Bowie in issuing this kind of intellectual property rights backed bond.

[62] Strictly speaking, corporate bonds are only bonds issued by companies (corporates). Country bonds are called *government bonds* or *sovereign bonds*.

Finance – Markets, Instruments & Investments

perhaps even cancel repayment of the nominal amount. The reason for such a failure to honor contractual obligations could be an outright bankruptcy or other slightly less serious reasons such as a temporary liquidity crunch. As the reader understands, any cancellation of debt repayments, regardless of its cause, is a serious blow to the lender. Most of the time, though, the loans to companies or countries are paid back on time. However, when they are not, the loss to the lender is usually considerable. Therefore, credit as an academic discipline deals, first and foremost, with *extreme* but *rare* events.

As a consequence of the nature of credit risk, i.e. the low probability of a huge loss coupled with the large probability of a small but certain positive return to the investment, the return distribution of a portfolio of corporate bonds is highly skewed. If we plotted it, it would have a very long tail to the left and a very limited upside to the right. Most of the bonds would pay back the loan (with interest) on time and only a few would actually default (due to bankruptcy or some other *credit event*). Since the loss to the lender would be substantial in those few cases where the borrower defaults, the return distribution is heavily skewed towards the left. The normal distribution cannot be used to approximate the actual distribution and the ordinary focus on the entire distribution (the mean and the variance etc.) is of less importance. Instead, most focus is put on the long negative tail and the likelihood of the borrower defaulting during the lifetime of the loan, i.e. the *probability of default, PD*.

The default probability is the most important measure of credit risk and in section 12.4, and to some extent in section 12.2, we will go more into how a lender may assess the size of this probability. In addition to the default probability, however, it is also important to estimate the actual amount of money lost in case the borrower defaults. Luckily, for the lender, in most defaults a significant share of the loan is typically retrieved by the lender. In the case of bankruptcy, for instance, a liquidation of the bankrupt firm would normally generate means that could be used for repayment. The amount recovered, as a percentage of

© The Author and Studentlitteratur

the entire loan amount, is called the *recovery rate, RR*. If one minus the recovery rate (also-called the *loss given default*) is multiplied by the default probability, we end up with the *expected loss, EL*, of the bond:

$$EL = PD \cdot (1 - RR)$$
(12.1)

The expected loss of a particular loan or bond is crucial information for any debt investor. The expected loss has to be compensated for with a (credit) risk premium, and the way it is incorporated in the analysis is through the credit spread. The larger the expected loss, the larger the required credit spread. In fact, in our somewhat simplified analysis we can equate the two as follows

$$r_{corporate-bond} - r_f = EL$$
(12.2)

That is, the interest rate paid by the corporate borrower will be higher than the risk-free interest rate, r_f. Exactly how much higher will depend on the expected loss caused by a possible future default. Of course, the *typical* loss for the lender will be zero! In most cases, perhaps 95 out of 100 loans or so, the borrower will *not* default. The most common loss will therefore be zero. However, in those few rare cases when the borrower actually *does* default, the loss will be very large, maybe as large as 70-80%. Therefore, the *expected* loss, i.e. the average loss, is positive and not equal to zero (as for the risk-free bond).

In the following example, taken from chapter 5, we will show how it all works.

Example 12.1
What is the price of a 10-year zero-coupon bond issued by the German company BÖCF? The nominal amount is 1 million Euro. The risk-free interest rate is 3%, and on top of that the lender requires an additional credit risk premium, the credit spread. In chapter 5 we assumed that this risk premium had been estimated by the investor/lender to be 2%, but we did not discuss how this premium was estimated. Here, though, we have

Finance – Markets, Instruments & Investments

stressed that the risk premium should be equal to the expected loss. The expected loss, in turn, is calculated using estimates of the 10-year default probability and the recovery rate. We assume that these parameters have been estimated by the investor: PD = 8% and RR = 75%. That is, the probability of BÖCF defaulting at some point within the next 10 years is estimated to be 8%, and, in case this happens, the amount that can be expected to be retrieved from a liquidation of the company is 75%. The expected loss due to default is therefore 8% • (1–0.75) = 2% and, consequently, the price the investor is prepared to pay for the corporate bond is

$$P_{Zero} = \frac{N}{\left(1+r_{corporate-bond}\right)^{10}} = \frac{N}{\left(1+r_f + EL\right)^{10}} = \frac{1000000}{\left(1+0.03+0.02\right)^{10}} \approx 614000 \text{ Euro}$$

Obviously, the investor will pay less for the corporate bond issued by BÖCF than for an identical bond issued by the German government and the reason is the credit risk of BÖCF. If it were not for the extra 2% interest rate offered by BÖCF, the lender would not be prepared to lend to BÖCF. The reason is a likelihood of 8 out of 100 that BÖCF will go bankrupt (instead of paying an annual interest rate of 5%) and 25% of the loan will be lost. There is no reason to expect a lender to ignore this quite substantial risk.

What makes the entire exercise particularly interesting is the investors' general difficulty in estimating the expected loss, and the possibilities this offers the skilled investor who, at least approximately, will manage to estimate EL. We will discuss this issue briefly in section 12.4.

In the example above, the probability of default is 8% and the recovery rate 75%. In reality, the probability of default varies over a very wide range across firms and across the business cycle; from lows around perhaps 0.01% for the safest companies in booming economies to highs of perhaps 50% for risky companies in recessions. This wide variation in default likelihood, even within the same industrial sector or geographic region, is one of the reasons for the huge interest in models and techniques for PD estimation. Meanwhile, the recovery rate, although time-varying and firm-dependent, varies much less. Typical values range from lows around 10%-20% to highs around 80%-90%. The recovery

© The Author and Studentlitteratur

rate also depends very much on something called the *seniority* of the debt instrument at hand. Companies often issue several different bonds with different seniority (subordinate, senior unsecured, senior secured etc.) where the only difference relates to the repayment hierarchy in case of bankruptcy. Essentially, in bankruptcy, the senior debt holders receive their money before the more junior claimants. This is the reason for the lower recovery rate for subordinate bonds, everything else equal, compared to senior bonds. Consequently, junior bonds pay higher interest rates than senior ones.

Finally, it is worth stressing that not only loan and bond investors (lenders) are exposed to credit risk. Stockholders are also exposed to the risk of a company going bankrupt. In fact, in case of bankruptcy, the stockholders are even more junior in the hierarchy than the holders of subordinate bonds; the stockholders are only repaid after all the junior debt holders are repaid in full. Other investors, such as call option buyers or oil forward speculators are also exposed to credit risk. This time it is the counterparty that constitutes the credit risk. If your (long) call option is deep in-the-money, then it can very well be impossible for the counterparty to honor the contract. Bankruptcy is the only option and you as the option holder suffer a significant loss (or at least you lose a potential profit).

Finance – Markets, Instruments & Investments

12.2 Credit Rating Agencies

For almost one hundred years now, two US based companies, Moody's and Standard & Poor's, have rated companies and governments according to their ability to repay a loan. The firms are called *credit rating agencies* and their ratings are called *credit ratings*. Such ratings are of the utmost importance for any company that wishes to issue bonds in the capital market and the higher (better) the credit rating a company is given by the rating agencies the lower the borrowing rate it typically has to pay. Credit ratings are based on qualitative information (management quality, asset quality, liquidity situation) as well as quantitative information (stock market valuations, debt levels) that is collected by the rating agencies. The exact "formula" behind the calculation is secret.

There are only three major credit rating agencies (Fitch is the name of the third) and this has caused some observers to complain about a possible oligopoly situation. This criticism is probably relevant, not least considering the increased importance of credit ratings in the new Basel II rules (see section 12.3). Another reason for the criticism is the actual business model of the rating agencies; the rating agencies charge companies to be rated and this opens up for the possibility of rating agencies linking the credit rating of the company to the payment. On the other hand, the entire business idea of the rating agencies relies on the market having confidence in their ratings, and it is therefore quite unlikely that the rating agencies would relax their standards for a quick buck.

All the (three) rating agencies have similar rating scales. They are made up of around 20 (discrete) ratings, from the highest rating, called AAA (or Aaa), which indicates a company or government very far from default, to the lowest, called C (or D), which indicates a company or government on the brink of default. A list of the various credit ratings of the three major rating agencies is shown in Table 12.1.

© The Author and Studentlitteratur

Finance – Markets, Instruments & Investments

Standard & Poor's	Moody's	Fitch
AAA	Aaa	AAA
AA+	Aa1	AA+
AA	Aa2	AA
AA–	Aa3	AA–
A+	A1	A+
A	A2	A
A–	A3	A–
BBB+	Baa1	BBB+
BBB	Baa2	BBB
BBB–	Baa3	BBB–
-----	-----	-----
BB+	Ba1	BB+
BB	Ba2	BB
BB–	Ba3	BB–
B+	B1	B+
B	B2	B
B–	B3	B–
CCC+	Caa1	CCC+
CCC	Caa2	CCC
CCC–	Caa3	CCC–
CC	Ca	CC
C	C	C
D		D

Table 12.1 Rating scales of the three major rating agencies.

The rating of a company often changes over time. For instance, if a company is issuing too much debt (it is borrowing too much money) or if it encounters any other kind of problem that could affect its future ability to repay its debt (i.e., that increases its default probability), it is typically downgraded by the rating agencies. Rating downgrades and upgrades are fairly infrequent events that are conducted, say, once a year or once every two years. Again, this is sometimes used as criticism of the rating agencies; they are considered to be slow in their reaction to developments in the company's actual creditworthiness.

© The Author and Studentlitteratur

Finance – Markets, Instruments & Investments

One would expect a fairly close relationship between a company's credit rating and its credit spread, and that the various rating agencies would rank a set of firms in an almost identical fashion. That is, the relative creditworthiness of a group of firms should be evaluated similarly by the three agencies. Empirically, however, these results are not always observed. This is not very surprising considering that creditworthiness evaluation is far from being an exact science. On average, however, AAA-firms pay a very low credit spread on their bonds (perhaps 0.5%) while lower rated firms, such as CC- or CCC-firms pay a significant spread over the risk-free rate (perhaps 5-10%).

All ratings at or above BBB– (Baa3) are called investment grade ratings while those below BBB– are called non-investment grade or speculative grade ratings. While no company wants to be downgraded it is particularly bad for BBB– companies. The reason is that certain groups of investors, such as pension funds and insurance companies, are sometimes prevented from investing in speculative grade debt. This causes the price of downgraded BBB– bonds to fall disproportionally in value once the boundary between investment grade and non-investment grade is crossed. To make matters even worse, the drop in value is sometimes further aggravated by other investors' attempts to front-run any possible downgrading.

There is a myriad of different types of ratings. Banks and financial companies, for instance, are rated by the rating agencies in a slightly different way to ordinary non-financial firms. In addition to the rating of companies, the agencies rate governments and complex structured debt products (such as CDOs and CPDOs, see section 12.5). The ratings are further divided into long-term and short-term ratings, depending on the horizon of the creditworthiness-evaluation. Finally, in addition to company-level ratings there are issue-specific ratings, i.e. ratings associated with a certain bond issue.

In the following section we will discuss the new capital requirement rules suggested by the *Basel Committee for Banking Supervision*. These rules are about to be implemented in many of the more advanced economies and in this context the rating agencies are expected to have an additional important role to play in the future (as will be discussed briefly in the next section). To sum up, credit rating agencies are very important players in the world of credit.

12.3 The Basel II Regulatory Framework

Banks and other financial firms differ from non-financial firms in several ways. One difference is that banks are much more important to the general economy than ordinary firms; as an example, if a major Wall Street bank collapses it will be a much greater disaster for the US economy than if a major Detroit automobile company was going bankrupt. Another important difference, which is also relevant to this chapter on credit risk, is the significant risk of crisis contagion among banks (a domino effect that is sometimes called systemic risk); if one bank defaults, the close relationships of banks make other banks highly vulnerable to default as well. This is due to both significant inter-bank lending and possible bank runs where individuals start to withdraw their deposits from all banks as a precaution following the collapse of a single bank.

As a result of the interdependencies of banks and the critical importance of having a well-functioning banking system in any market economy, most governments regulate their domestic banks. This means that banks have to report to special government agencies that regulate and supervise the banking sector (*regulatory and supervisory agencies*). In the UK, for instance, the government body that regulates banks is the *Financial Services Authority* (FSA) and in Sweden it is *Finansinspektionen*. More generally, these institutions, together with their central banks, are responsible for the *financial stability* in the country. And to promote stability and order in the financial system, these institutions design rules and regulations that banks are forced to follow.

Due to the extent of international linkages of banks in today's global financial system, national regulators cooperate extensively with regulators in other countries. One forum for this cooperation is the *Basel*

Finance – Markets, Instruments & Investments

Committee on Banking Supervision (*The Basel Committee*) which meets at the *Bank for International Settlements* (BIS) in Basel, Switzerland. One result of the international cooperation in the Basel Committee is a set of *regulatory frameworks* developed for the countries involved (basically all the richest countries in the world). These frameworks are supposed to create a level playing field where banks in different countries are subjected to similar regulation. One of the more important items that are regulated in this way is the amount of capital that banks are required to hold. Basically, if a bank lends $100 million, it has to keep a certain share of that capital (perhaps $8 million) as equity (as a buffer against bank runs etc.). As a result, a bank cannot simply blow up its balance sheet arbitrarily to make more money on the gap between the borrowing rate and the lending rate. There is simply a limit to the amount of money the bank is allowed to lend.

The first regulatory framework developed by the Basel Committee was called *Basel I*. This was a rather simple set of rules and it left banks with ample opportunities to circumvent the regulations (*regulatory arbitrage*). The regulatory framework was also very much a one-size-fits-all set of rules and this left some banks over-regulated and some under-regulated. To limit the opportunities for banks to succeed in circumventing the regulations, and to align the capital requirement for a certain bank to its actual risk level, the Basel Committee has recently developed a new framework called *Basel II*. With a start in 2007, the Basel II rules are about to be implemented in many of the most advanced countries.

Credit risk is the most significant risk in a typical bank, and the capital requirements mentioned above therefore focus particularly on this risk. It is also the main reason for us to treat regulation of banks in this chapter. The important issue here is that in the new set of rules defined by Basel II, the banks will be left with much more flexibility to choose their own capital levels. The rules will not be the old one-size-fits-all rules anymore, but they will be dependent on the actual (credit) risk that the bank is exposed to. The more risky banks will have to set aside more capital than before, while the less risky ones will get away with less

© *The Author and Studentlitteratur*

181

capital requirements. On average, however, the level of capital is supposed to be more or less unchanged.

One of the interesting issues about Basel II is that the banks themselves will be allowed to calculate the credit risk on which the capital requirements will be based. Of course, the banks will be checked afterwards (so-called *backtesting*) and if they systematically underestimate their own risk they will be punished with harder regulation in the future. Another, related, issue is the flexibility left to the banks in choosing methods to calculate this risk. Some banks, particularly the smaller or less advanced ones, will use *credit ratings* to assess their credit risk exposure and this will increase the importance of the rating agencies. Other banks, particularly the larger or more advanced ones, will use advanced models to calculate actual *expected losses* (*EL*). This model-dependency of the Basel II regulatory framework is one important reason for the extensive development of credit risk models over the last five to ten years. Basel II is also one of many factors behind the fast growth in credit, which is why two pages are devoted to discussing this institutional issue in this book on markets and instruments.

12.4 Credit Risk Models

In section 12.3, we discussed the Basel II set of rules and its importance for the development of modern *credit risk models*. Basel II is only one reason for the recent surge in models used to price and manage credit risk, however. Other important reasons are increased counterparty credit risk levels caused by increased over-the-counter trading, particularly in off-balance-sheet derivatives, an increase in defaults around the turn of the century, and advances in computer and communications technology.

As recently as 10 to 20 years ago, credit ratings and so-called *credit scoring models* were the most common (objective) ways of measuring

Finance – Markets, Instruments & Investments

credit risk and of evaluating potential borrowers.[63] Credit scoring models typically use accounting information from a firm's balance sheet to assess its likelihood of defaulting on its debt. By weighting together important parameters such as sales-to-assets ratios, working capital-to-assets ratios and debt-to-equity ratios into an overall *score* (number), the lender can decide if the borrower is creditworthy or not. The exact weighting procedure is motivated by statistical arguments and many different scores with different parameters and weighting choices exist.

One problem with credit scores is that both the parameter choice and the weighting-choice *lack a robust theoretical underpinning*. There is no financial theory implying the simple linear combination of a certain set of accounting variables used in the credit score. In addition, the credit score shares many of the problems of the credit ratings offered by the major rating agencies. First, both the scores and the ratings are *relative* measures of credit risk; when you use ratings or scores, you cannot tell how risky a particular borrower is; only how much riskier this borrower is compared to other borrowers. Second, there is *no obvious interpretation* of either the score or the rating; what does an AA rating or a credit score equal to 5 actually mean? Third, the focus on *individual borrowers* makes it difficult to calculate the credit risk of an entire portfolio of credit risky loans or bonds; there is no room for default contagion/correlation in the classical rating or scoring systems. Fourth, ratings and scores are inherently *backward looking* since they are based on "old" information; when you calculate a score you use information from the balance sheet and this information may be many months old. The same holds for rating agencies that cannot update the ratings on a daily, or even monthly, basis.

All the abovementioned problems with the traditional credit risk measurement approaches have spurred the development of more advanced credit risk models. These so-called modern credit models are used both for risk management purposes and for the pricing of all kinds

---

[63] Subjective opinions of senior bank officials have of course always been important for the lending decision as well.

© *The Author and Studentlitteratur*

Finance – Markets, Instruments & Investments

of credit-risky instruments (not only loans and bonds). Among the different families of modern credit risk models (reduced form models, structural models, insurance-based models, macro-models) the *structural model* family stands out as particularly elegant and simple. While the *reduced form models* might be better for some purposes, the structural models are more common in commercial credit risk packages.

The structural models for measuring credit risk (also-called contingent claims models) are all based on a beautiful model suggested by Robert C. Merton in 1974. This model is nowadays simply known as the Merton-model and is directly based on the Black-Scholes model. Merton, ingeniously, realized that the stock of an ordinary company can be seen as a call option on the total assets of the company, with a strike price equal to the total debt of the company. Basically, the stockholders are entitled to the residual that remains after the debt (strike price) is repaid, and they have the option to walk away from the company if the debt exceeds the asset value. With this model it is fairly straightforward to calculate the probability of default (*PD*) needed for bond pricing etc. Needless to say, this is an enormous step forward compared to ratings and scores that cannot easily be used for pricing purposes. Moreover, the Merton-model lends itself very well to portfolio modeling, and expected losses of entire credit portfolios can be calculated. Besides, since the *PD* is calculated using forward looking market information (from the stock market), it reacts much faster to credit deteriorations/improvements. Finally, it should be mentioned that the Merton model has been (successfully) implemented commercially, for instance by the firm KMV. Interestingly, Moody's, the rating agency, bought KMV in 2002 and nowadays the firm is known as Moody's|KMV. In a way, this purchase can be taken as evidence of the appearance of new and better ways of evaluating the creditworthiness of borrowers. There are simply some new kids on the block now!

Finance – Markets, Instruments & Investments

12.5 Credit Derivatives

One of the most interesting developments in finance over the last decade is the advent of the *credit derivative*. In earlier chapters, we encountered two basic types of derivatives, namely forwards/futures and options. These derivatives contract types have been around for a very long time. Credit derivatives, on the other hand, are a very new family of derivatives contracts. Instead of having an ordinary financial asset such as a company stock or a barrel of oil as an underlying asset, credit derivatives have some kind of default-related event as the underlying asset. The typical underlying asset is an outright bankruptcy and the archetype of a credit derivative is an insurance contract against a company going bankrupt.

The most common credit derivative is the *credit default swap* (CDS) and it is designed to function exactly like the insurance contract mentioned above.[64] If the underlying firm, for instance the earlier mentioned company BÖCF, were to file for bankruptcy, the holder of the BÖCF CDS contract, $CDS_{BÖCF}$, would be fully protected against the bankruptcy. Regardless of his/her current exposure to BÖCF (as a lender, stockholder or other counterparty) the owner of the $CDS_{BÖCF}$ contract could rest assured that he/she would be compensated for any losses caused by the *credit event*. The seller of the $CDS_{BÖCF}$ contract, on the other hand, would have to reimburse the holder with an amount identical to the loss due to the bankruptcy (remember, a positive recovery rate often makes this amount substantially smaller than the nominal amount of the exposure). Of course, as a compensation for providing the default protection, the seller of the CDS contract receives a fee from the CDS buyer (compare the option premium in chapter 8). This fee is typically paid on an annual or semi-annual basis and it is known as the *CDS spread*.[65]

---

[64] Around half the volume in the global credit derivatives trading is made up of single-name CDS contracts (in 2006).

[65] The size of the CDS spread is almost identical to the corporate bond credit spread discussed earlier.

© *The Author and Studentlitteratur*

Finance – Markets, Instruments & Investments

As described above, the CDS contract resembles an ordinary insurance contract. One important difference, however, is that the CDS contract may be bought or sold in a liquid (secondary) market. While ordinary insurance contracts typically are non-traded contracts, CDS contracts are easy to trade on a frequent basis. In fact, it is as common to take a short position in the creditworthiness of the underlying firm (buy the CDS) as a long position (sell the CDS). This has made it possible for investors to bet on a firm's creditworthiness deteriorating, not only improving. Compare this to ordinary corporate bonds. If you expect the firm issuing the bond to be less likely to default in the future, then it is a good idea to buy the bond. But, what if you expect the default likelihood of the firm to increase? Traditionally, you would have had to short the corporate bond (borrow it from someone else, sell it in the market, and return it to the original owner in the future) and this was both difficult and expensive. Nowadays, however, with the advent of the CDS market, the investor simply buys a CDS contract and the closer the firm gets to default the more valuable the CDS gets. If the investor sells the CDS at this stage, he/she makes a profit similar to an investor who buys a stock at a low price and sells it at a higher price to make a profit. It is developments like these that have made credit become an asset class in its own right!

In addition to the introduction of the CDS contract in the early 2000s, many other credit derivatives and credit derivatives-like structures have been introduced over the last five years or so. One example is the *synthetic collateralized debt obligation* (CDO). To understand how these contracts work we have to start by briefly explaining what an ordinary collateralized debt obligation (CDO) is. Ordinary CDOs, also-called cash CDOs, have been around for some twenty years and they are asset-backed securities where the securities backing the CDO could be any kind of asset (examples are loans, corporate bonds, other CDOs, microloans etc.).[66] If you buy a CDO, it is like buying a corporate bond.

---

[66] One interesting development is the application of the CDO technology/methodology to microcredit; instead of backing the CDO with ordinary bonds and loans, one can stuff the CDO with thousands of microloans! Microloans are

Finance – Markets, Instruments & Investments

You are promised a certain set of future cashflows (coupons) plus the nominal amount, but just like corporate bonds, however, the CDO contains credit risk; it is not 100% sure that you will get your money back. A CDO differs from an ordinary corporate bond in providing the investor with a choice; the CDO contains different classes (*tranches*) and it is up to the investor to choose the classes that suit him or her. Some tranches are more risky, and promise a high interest rate, while some are close to risk-free, and therefore pay an interest rate just slightly above the risk-free interest rate. So, just like a vineyard typically produces wine of different quality and price, a CDO offers a set of debt instruments with different creditworthiness and interest rates. The invention of the CDS contract has speeded up the development of the CDO market significantly since someone realized that one could back the CDO with CDS contracts instead of with corporate loans or bonds. This is the synthetic CDO; an ordinary CDO but with CDS contracts backing the different CDO tranches. Since CDS contracts nowadays are easier to come by than classic bonds, the synthetic CDO is easier to set up and more flexible in its nature. The increased demand for synthetic CDOs has, in turn, increased the demand for CDS contracts and in a way the two markets fuel each other!

Finally, it should be mentioned that there is very little evidence of the growth of the credit derivatives market losing pace. Each year, new contract types are introduced. One of the more successful recent developments is the introduction of tradable *CDS indexes*. In 2004, the *iTraxx* CDS indexes in Europe and Asia and the *CDX* CDS indexes in the US were introduced. These have been among the fastest growing financial markets since their introduction in 2004, and today a significant share of the total CDS volume is in these *multi-name CDS contracts*. Furthermore, in 2007, exchange traded *CDS index futures* contracts

---

loans to poor people (typical loan size is $100-$1000) and the CDO methodology may make it possible to extend more credit to these people. Basically, the microfinance CDO would help channel money from the rich to the poor.

© The Author and Studentlitteratur

Finance – Markets, Instruments & Investments

written on the *iTraxx* indexes were introduced.[67] This move could be a significant step in the direction of commoditizing credit in the way equity has been commoditized over the last century. Other interesting developments have followed in the footsteps of the CDS indexes. *Constant Proportion Debt Obligations,* CPDOs, for instance, try to create a leveraged investment in a CDS index within an interesting contract structure.[68] Basically, a CPDO is a leveraged bet on a pool of CDS contracts (current CPDOs use the CDS indexes mentioned above). The leverage is increased when you make a loss, and the instrument promises a return in line with high-risk corporate bonds. Despite this, and despite an average BBB credit rating of the underlying names, the structure has been given a AAA rating by some of the major rating agencies. The debate (as of early 2007) is about whether this is too good to be true! As always, only the future can tell...

12.6 Summary

In this chapter we have discussed an asset class, credit, which is closely related to another asset class, namely debt. Credit is currently one of the fastest growing fields of finance, and credit and credit risk are important to all investors, whether about debt or equity investments. Essentially, the basic idea is that any counterparty, be it a borrower or a counterparty in a derivatives contract, might fail to fulfill his or her contractual obligations. It may be a bond issuer that is late with interest rate payments or a put option seller that goes bankrupt. In any case, this risk, called credit risk, is important for all investors. While credit risk management traditionally was limited to loan and bond investors requiring an additional risk premium, the credit spread, on top of the risk-free interest rate, credit risk management today is also extended to equity and derivatives investors more generally. Furthermore, while, the major rating agencies Moody's and Standard & Poor's were traditionally

---

[67] These are the first exchange traded credit derivatives. All other credit derivatives are traded over-the-counter.

[68] Not to be confused with another golden boy called C3PO.....

188   *© The Author and Studentlitteratur*

Finance – Markets, Instruments & Investments

the sole providers of credit risk assessments, there are currently other, more model-based, approaches to credit risk measurement. Finally, one of the more interesting recent developments in this area is the introduction of credit derivatives on a large scale. With these instruments investors not only protect themselves against credit risk, but may also speculate on the improving or deteriorating creditworthiness of firms and governments. As a result of all this, credit is quickly becoming an asset class of its own!

Appendix:
Basic Mathematical Statistics

To fully appreciate this textbook, a basic understanding of the most fundamental principles of mathematical statistics is required. This appendix lists and briefly describes the most important statistical concepts used in this book. It is far from a complete description of basic mathematical statistics, and is only included to give the reader the bare essentials of statistical knowledge. Hopefully, many readers will already be familiar with the material and for them the appendix could serve as a short reminder of what should be kept in mind when reading the rest of the book.

A.1 Random Variables

If you roll an ordinary die, you know that the number of dots (pips) that you roll is uncertain. In statistical language, *the number of dots* is a *random variable* (*stochastic variable*). This is different from many other variables, such as your age, which clearly is not a random variable since you always know in advance what your age will be at a certain date. Such variables are called *deterministic variables*.

If we return to random variables, they may be divided into discrete and continuous random variables. The number of dots rolled using a die is a discrete random variable since the number of outcomes is finite (if it is a traditional six-sided die, the number of outcomes is equal to six). The height of an average female student, on the other hand, is a continuous random variable since the number of possible outcomes is infinite (unless we measure the height in discrete steps, such as centimeters).

© The Author and Studentlitteratur

A.2 Probability Distributions

The probability distribution of a random variable tells us the possible outcomes *and* what their probabilities are. The number of dots in the die roll above is a discrete random variable and the probability distribution is simply represented by the six outcomes and their individual probabilities of being the realized outcome. If the die is an ordinary six-sided die, then each of these six outcomes would have a probability of *1/6* (i.e., *0.16667*). If this was not the case, then the die would be useless for all normal purposes. It would be a crooked die and the only people appreciating it would be gamblers with the intention of cheating. The probability distribution of a normal die is shown in Figure A.1 and that of a crooked die is shown in Figure A.2.

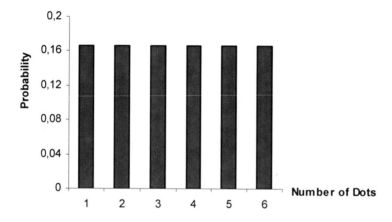

Figure A.1 The probability distribution of a normal six-sided die.

Finance — Markets, Instruments & Investments

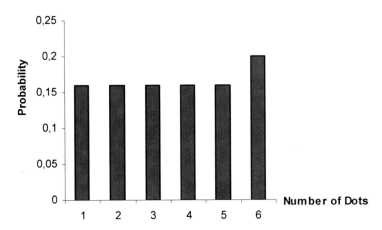

Figure A.2 The probability distribution of a crooked six-sided die.

In the case of the die, the probability distribution is represented by six outcomes with equal probabilities, but most random variables (discrete or not) do not have outcomes with equal probabilities. For example, think of the result in a football match. The result can only be win, loss or tie, and the probabilities of these three states are of course not equal to 1/3 each. Instead, one of the teams is typically better than the other team, and the probability of the better team winning is higher than 1/3. The same holds for continuous distributions. Think of the temperature in your hometown, for example. Any day of the year, some temperatures are more likely than others. In any case, if you sum up the probabilities of a random variable it will always sum up to one. That is, the probability of any of the outcomes being realized is equal to one (or 100%).

Although probability distributions can have any shape, some distributions are more common than others. The most commonly found distribution in the sciences, as well as in economics and finance, is the normal distribution. This distribution has the shape shown in Figure A.3 and it is a distribution that many familiar random variables follow. For instance, if the weight of all the male students in the UK was recorded and represented in a histogram, then this histogram would be very similar to the normal distribution. Similarly, many other phenomena in the natural and social sciences are (close to) normally distributed. And in finance, the normal distribution is by far the most common distribution to work with in models and in empirical investigations. In this introductory textbook, however, we will not (explicitly) use the normal distribution.

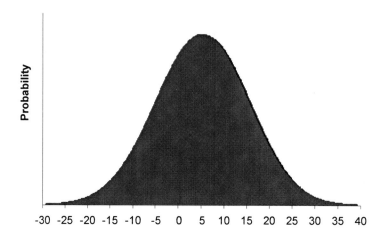

Figure A.3 The normal distribution, N(5,10), i.e. the normal distribution with mean = 5 and standard deviation = 10.

One nice feature of the normal distribution is that it is fully determined by its mean and standard deviation (or variance). The mean is the "center of gravity" of the distribution and the variance is the "width" of the distribution. In the next section we will discuss these two extremely important parameters.

A.3 Means and Variances

The *mean*, or *expected value*, μ, of a probability distribution X is given by the following expression

Finance – Markets, Instruments & Investments

$$\mu = E[X] = \sum_{i=1}^{n} p_i x_i$$

where x_i is outcome i and p_i is the probability of the same outcome. There is a total of n outcomes. The expression $E[X]$ is shorthand for the expected value of the probability distribution X.

If we apply this formula to the example with the die, then we get the following

$$\mu_{Die} = p_1 x_1 + p_2 x_2 + p_3 x_3 + p_4 x_4 + p_5 x_5 + p_6 x_6 =$$
$$= \frac{1}{6}1 + \frac{1}{6}2 + \frac{1}{6}3 + \frac{1}{6}4 + \frac{1}{6}5 + \frac{1}{6}6 = 3.5$$

In words, the expected value, or mean, of *the number of dots* is equal to 3.5, despite this value not even being a possible outcome. It simply means that if you throw the die one million times or so, the average number of dots will be 3.5.

The other important statistical parameter that we need to be familiar with is the *variance*, σ^2, of a probability distribution X

$$\sigma^2 = E\left[(X - \mu)^2\right] = \sum_{i=1}^{n} p_i (x_i - \mu)^2$$

where, again, x_i is outcome i and p_i is the probability of the same outcome. This time the expectation is the expectation of the squared deviation from the mean of X. Therefore, in order to calculate the variance, we first need to estimate the mean.

The mean and the variance are related to each other. They are the first two so-called *moments* of the probability distribution X. The square-root of the variance, in turn, is called the *standard deviation*, σ. The standard deviation is at least as commonly found in financial models as the variance, and both measures quantify the "range" or "width" of possible

© *The Author and Studentlitteratur*

Finance – Markets, Instruments & Investments

outcomes. The more spread out the probability distribution, or the more likely the more extreme outcomes, the larger the variance (standard deviation).

If we want to calculate the variance of a die, then we get the following result

$$\sigma^2_{Die} = p_1(x_1 - \mu)^2 + p_2(x_2 - \mu)^2 + p_3(x_3 - \mu)^2 + p_4(x_4 - \mu)^2 + p_5(x_5 - \mu)^2 + p_6(x_6 - \mu)^2 =$$
$$= \frac{1}{6}(1 - 3.5)^2 + \frac{1}{6}(2 - 3.5)^2 + \frac{1}{6}(3 - 3.5)^2 + \frac{1}{6}(4 - 3.5)^2 + \frac{1}{6}(5 - 3.5)^2 + \frac{1}{6}(6 - 3.5)^2 \approx 2.92$$

The standard deviation, in turn, of the ordinary die is equal to $\sqrt{2.92} \approx$ 1.71. This is a quantitative measure of the *range* of possible outcomes of an ordinary die. If the die had had the outcomes 1,3,5,7,9,11 instead of 1,2,3,4,5,6, then the variance (standard deviation) would have been much higher.

A.4 Correlation

The correlation between two random variables is a measure of how the two random variables co-vary (co-move). For example, think about two dice. If one of the dice always returns a large number of dots *when* the other die returns a large number of dots, the two (magic?) dice are said to have *positively correlated* outcomes. If the situation is reversed, i.e. if one die always behaves in the opposite way to the other, then the two dice have *negatively correlated* outcomes. In real life, however, two dice are typically *uncorrelated*, i.e. the number of dots on one die has nothing to do with the number of dots on the other die. The two dice have zero correlation.

To quantify the degree of co-variation, one has to define the so-called *correlation coefficient, ρ,* which is a parameter that needs to be estimated just like the mean or the variance. The correlation coefficient is normalized (in size) and it cannot take on values larger than one or lower than minus one, i.e. $-1 \leq \rho \leq 1$. If the correlation between two variables

196   © *The Author and Studentlitteratur*

Finance – Markets, Instruments & Investments

is +1 (or –1), then the two random variables are said to be perfectly correlated (or perfectly negatively correlated).

To calculate the correlation coefficient one first has to calculate the *covariance*, $\sigma_{A,B}$. The covariance is related to the variance but it involves two random variables, rather than merely one. The covariance between two random variables A and B is quantified in the following way (notice the similarity between this expression and the expression for the variance)

$$\sigma_{A,B} = E\big[(A - \mu_A)(B - \mu_B)\big] = \sum_{i=1}^{n} p_i(x_{i,A} - \mu_A)(x_{i,B} - \mu_B)$$

and the correlation coefficient is given by the following expression involving the covariance and the two random variables' standard deviations

$$\rho_{A,B} = \frac{\sigma_{A,B}}{\sigma_A \sigma_B}$$

If we were to calculate the correlation, or the covariance, between two of the ordinary dice discussed above we would get a value equal to zero. The reason is of course that the number of dots on two separate dice are two completely independent random variables without any co-variation.

A.5 Just Another Example

Imagine two stocks, AA and BB. The future returns of these two stocks are two random variables, and their outcomes (returns) depend on the world business cycle as follows:

Business Cycle	Probability	Return AA (%)	Return BB (%)
Recession	1/3	0	5
Normal	1/3	5	15
Expansion	1/3	10	–5

© *The Author and Studentlitteratur*

Finance – Markets, Instruments & Investments

That is, each stock can take on one of three different prices in the future. The AA stock behaves like a typical business-cycle sensitive stock while the BB stock has a more complicated relationship with the business cycle. For some reason, the BB stock performs best when the business cycle is normal.

The means (expected values) of the two stocks' returns are easily calculated as

$$\mu_{AA} = \frac{1}{3}0 + \frac{1}{3}5 + \frac{1}{3}10 = 5$$

$$\mu_{BB} = \frac{1}{3}5 + \frac{1}{3}15 + \frac{1}{3}(-5) = 5$$

Obviously, both stocks have the same mean return, i.e. 5%.

The mean only tells us what the "average" return of the stock is. It tells us nothing about the uncertainty of this return; since the two returns are random variables we cannot be sure about the return being 5%. In fact, nothing says that the return will be exactly 5%. In this particular example the outcome 5% is actually possible, but it is easy to imagine examples where the mean is different from all the possible outcomes (see the die example above, for instance).

To get an estimate of how "uncertain" the two returns are we calculate their variances. The variance is the most common way of quantifying the *range* of possible outcomes

$$\sigma^2{}_{AA} = \frac{1}{3}(0-5)^2 + \frac{1}{3}(5-5)^2 + \frac{1}{3}(10-5)^2 = \frac{50}{3}$$

$$\sigma^2{}_{BB} = \frac{1}{3}(5-5)^2 + \frac{1}{3}(15-5)^2 + \frac{1}{3}(-5-5)^2 = \frac{200}{3}$$

We have now quantified the variability in the two stock returns and are able to say that the BB stock shows four times as much variability as the

198   © *The Author and Studentlitteratur*

Finance – Markets, Instruments & Investments

AA stock. More exactly, the variance of the BB stock return distribution is four times that of the AA stock return distribution. In this simple example, it was of course not necessary to calculate the variances to make this observation. It is quite clear just from looking at the possible outcomes that the BB stock is more "uncertain". The range of possible BB stock returns (–5 – 15) is wider than that of possible AA stock returns (0 – 10).

Finally, we want to quantify the degree of covariation of the two stock returns. From a quick visual investigation of the possible outcomes the answer would probably be that the two stocks have a somewhat *negative* association with each other; after all, the BB stock's *best* performance coincides with the AA stock's *worst* performance. To quantify this observation in numbers, we calculate the correlation coefficient. However, to do that we first need to calculate the covariance

$$\sigma^2_{AA,BB} = \frac{1}{3}(0-5)(5-5)+\frac{1}{3}(5-5)(15-5)+\frac{1}{3}(10-5)(-5-5)=\frac{-50}{3}$$

From the covariance and the two standard deviations we can immediately calculate the correlation coefficient as

$$\rho_{AA,BB} = \frac{\dfrac{-50}{3}}{\sqrt{\dfrac{50}{3}}\sqrt{\dfrac{200}{3}}} = -0.5$$

In other words, what we observed visually is now confirmed by the mathematics. The two stocks are negatively correlated with each other.

© The Author and Studentlitteratur

References

Black, F. and Scholes, M., 1973, The Pricing of Options and Corporate Liabilities. *Journal of Political Economy* 81 (3), 637-654.

Bodie, Z. and Merton, R.C., 2000, *Finance*. New Jersey: Prentice Hall.

Brealey, R. and Myers, C., 2003, *Principles of corporate finance*. New York: McGraw-Hill.

Crouhy, M., Mark R., and Galai, D., 2000, *Risk management*. New York: McGraw-Hill.

Fabozzi, F.J., 2004, *Bond markets, analysis, and strategies*. New Jersey: Pearson Education.

Howells, P. and Bain, K., 2007, *Financial markets and institutions*. Essex: Pearson Education.

Hull, J., 2005, *Options, futures and other derivatives*. New Jersey: Prentice Hall.

Lintner, J., 1965, The valuation of risk assets and the selection of risky investments in stock portfolios and capital budgets, *Review of economics and statistics*, 47, 13-37.

Malkiel, B.G., 2007, *A Random walk down Wall Street: the time-tested strategy for successful investing*. New York: W. W. Norton.

Markowitz, H.M., 1974, Portfolio selection, *Journal of Finance*, 7, 77-91.

Merton, R.C., 1974, On the Pricing of Corporate Debt: The Risk Structure of Interest Rates, *Journal of Finance*, 29, 449-470.

Pike, R. and Neale, B., 2007, *Corporate finance and investments*. Essex: Pearson Education.

Finance – Markets, Instruments & Investments

Pilbeam, K., 2005, *Finance and financial markets*. London: Palgrave Macmillan.

Ross, S.A., Westerfield R.W., and Jaffe, J., 2006, *Corporate finance*. New York: McGraw-Hill.

Saunders, A. and Allen, L., 2001, *Credit risk measurement: new approaches to value at risk and other paradigms*. New York: Wiley.

Sharpe, W.F., 1985, *Investments*. New Jersey: Prentice Hall.

Sharpe, W.F., 1964, Capital asset prices: a theory of market equilibrium under conditions of risk, *Journal of Finance*, 19, 425-442.

Varian, H.L., 1987, The arbitrage principle in financial economics, *Economic Perspectives*, 1 (2), 55-72.

Subject Index

American option, 104
annuity, 57, 64
arbitrage, 40
arbitrageur, 41
arbitrage principle, 40
at-the-money, 106

bank, 18
Basel II, 180
behavioral finance, 81
beta-value (β), 152
Black-Scholes option pricing
    formula. 122
bond, 21, 57
bond pricing, 61

call option, 24, 104
capital asset pricing model
    (CAPM), 145
capital market line (CML), 136,
    149
cash settlement, 88
collateralized debt obligation
    (CDO), 22, 186
commodity, 23
compounding, 29
corporate bonds, 22, 70, 172
correlation, 128, 141, 196
coupon, 64
coupon bond, 63
credit, 21, 171

credit default swap (CDS), 22, 185
credit derivative, 22, 185
credit rating, 177
credit rating agency, 177
credit risk model, 182
credit spread, 172

debt, 21, 57, 172
default probability, 173
derivative, 85, 97, 185
discount, 62, 65
discounting, 31
diversifiable risk, 147
diversification, 53, 125, 147
dividend, 73, 76
dividend discount model, 76, 155

effective interest rate, 33
efficient frontier, 134
efficient market hypothesis, 164
equity, 22, 73
European option, 104
exchange, 20
exercise price, 103
expected return, 48

firm-specific risk, 147
fixed income, 21
foreign exchange, 22
forward, 24, 52, 85
forward pricing, 91

© The Author and Studentlitteratur

203

Finance – Markets, Instruments & Investments

fundamental analysis, 81
futures, 24, 52, 85
futures pricing, 90
future value, 29

government bond, 21, 70

hedge fund, 19
hedging, 52

insider, 160, 167
insurance, 53
insurance company, 19
in-the-money, 106
intrinsic value, 118
investment management firm, 19
investment portfolio choice, 125, 145

law of one price, 40
leverage, 20
long (position), 86

market portfolio, 148
market risk, 147
margin, 88
mark-to-market, 89
maturity, 59, 86, 103
mean return, 48

nominal amount, 62
non-diversifiable risk, 147
normal distribution, 51, 193

optimal portfolio, 138, 143, 149
option, 24, 53, 97
option premium, 101, 118
option pricing, 122
out-of-the-money, 106

over-the-counter (OTC), 20

par, 65
passive investment, 150
payoff diagram, 107
portfolio choice, 125, 145
portfolio frontier, 133
premium, 65
present value, 31
put-call parity, 114
put option, 104

real estate, 25
recovery rate, 174
regulation (of banks), 180
return, 27
risk-averse, 44
risk aversion, 45
risk-free asset, 28
risk-lover, 45
risk management, 52
risk measurement, 47
risk neutral, 45
risk premium, 152, 174
risky asset, 28

security market line (SML), 153
short (position), 86
simple interest rate, 34
spot, 24, 86
standard deviation, 47, 195
stock(s), 22, 73
stock index, 102
stock market anomalies, 167
stock pricing, 155
strike price, 103
systematic risk, 147

technical analysis, 81, 164

204

© *The Author and Studentlitteratur*

Finance – *Markets, Instruments & Investments*

time value (of money), 27
time value (of option), 118
treasury bond, 70
two-fund separation, 142

variance, 194
volatility, 47

zero-coupon bond, 61

Printed in the United States
145986LV00001B/164/P